PRAISE FOR ECLECTIC WITCHCRAFT

"*Eclectic Witchcraft* covers a plethora of modern magical topics that anyone can use as a foundation to create their own eclectic witchcraft practice. With numerous correspondence lists, tips, options, insights, and spells, this book will be especially helpful for new witches and witches in the broom closet who want to bring more magic to their everyday lives."

—Astrea Taylor, author of *Intuitive Witchcraft* and *Air Magic*

T0109523

eclectic witchcraft

about the author

Charlotte Wilde is the owner of the occult shop Eclectic Charge, cohost of the *Cosmic Cauldron* podcast, and an article contributor at Pagan Patheos. She is a lifelong student of the occult but, more specifically, a practicing eclectic folk witch whose practice centers around the use of natural materials to create magick and further her connection with divinity. Through her platforms, she teaches awakening or aspiring witches some of the fundamentals of witchcraft by sharing her knowledge gained through both research and rigorous trial and error. In her spare time, you can find her attempting to tackle her ever-growing TBR pile or ticking off travel destinations on her bucket list.

to write to the author

If you wish to contact the author or would like more information about this book, please write to the author in care of Llewellyn Worldwide Ltd. and we will forward your request. Both the author and the publisher appreciate hearing from you and learning of your enjoyment of this book and how it has helped you. Llewellyn Worldwide Ltd. cannot guarantee that every letter written to the author can be answered, but all will be forwarded. Please write to:

Charlotte Wilde
℅ Llewellyn Worldwide
2143 Wooddale Drive
Woodbury, MN 55125-2989
Please enclose a self-addressed stamped envelope for reply,
or $1.00 to cover costs. If outside the U.S.A., enclose
an international postal reply coupon.

Many of Llewellyn's authors have websites with additional
information and resources. For more information,
please visit our website at http://www.llewellyn.com.

CHARLOTTE WILDE

Old Ways
for
Modern
Magick

eclectic
witchcraft

Foreword by David Salisbury

Llewellyn Publications
Woodbury, Minnesota

FIRST EDITION
First Printing, 2023

Book design by Christine Ha
Cover design by Shannon McKuhen
Interior art (wheel of the year (page 32), tools (pages 50–57), (moon phases (page 84), runes (pages 148–151), natal chart (page 174), sun symbol (page 175), moon and ascendent symbols (page 176), Mercury and Venus symbols (page 177), Mars and Jupiter symbols (page 178), Saturn and Uranus symbols (page 179), Neptune and Pluto symbols (page 180), conjunction, sextile, trine, square, and opposition symbols and charts (pages 191–195), grand trine, kite, grand cross, yod, and t-square symbols (pages 193–197) by the Llewellyn Art Department

Llewellyn Publications is a registered trademark of Llewellyn Worldwide Ltd.

Library of Congress Cataloging-in-Publication Data (Pending)
ISBN: 978-0-7387-7456-5

Llewellyn Worldwide Ltd. does not participate in, endorse, or have any authority or responsibility concerning private business transactions between our authors and the public.

All mail addressed to the author is forwarded but the publisher cannot, unless specifically instructed by the author, give out an address or phone number.

Any internet references contained in this work are current at publication time, but the publisher cannot guarantee that a specific location will continue to be maintained. Please refer to the publisher's website for links to authors' websites and other sources.

Llewellyn Publications
A Division of Llewellyn Worldwide Ltd.
2143 Wooddale Drive
Woodbury, MN 55125-2989
www.llewellyn.com

Printed in the United States of America

DISCLaimeR

This book is intended to help assist you through your spiritual journey and aims to do so safely. Please be mindful when working with fire in any capacity to ensure that you are working on a firesafe surface with proper attire and utensils. We don't want any personal or property damage to occur on this journey. When using oils, please note that some are flammable. Regarding essential oils, be careful with direct contact on the skin, as they must be diluted with a carrier oil. While this book will guide you through the process of shadow work, remember that this is not a suitable replacement for therapy, and it works best in unison with proper medical care.

contents

Exercises
WITCHCRAFT
IN ACTION

foreword

*m*ateria magica is a charming esoteric phrase that generally describes the "stuff" that we work with in the many magical traditions out there. What usually comes to mind for most practitioners are the things we place on our altars and store within our witches' cabinets: herbs, stones, talismans, and other accoutrements. These are the fun objects that attract so many folks, myself included, to witchcraft to begin with. We humans are tactile creatures, and being able to work with spirited objects that can rest in the palms of our hands inspires us to creativity and connects us with the physicality of our magic.

And yet the witch also works with an enormous amount of materia that cannot fit so easily in our hands—or even be grasped at all. The crashing waves of the sea, the cleft rock of a mountain face, and even the countless stars of the cosmos are all material bodies that we learn to speak with and align our own powers to. One by one we open our eyes to the enormity of nature and the even more enormous legion of spirits and forces that reside within it. In this way, the work of becoming a witch is a long process of learning to see the world in a new way—in a way that recognizes the hidden potential of this vast reality we find ourselves in.

Once our eyes are open to the world, we can then begin to engage with it properly and with intention. In witchcraft we might use the term *ars magica* to describe this. It is the "skill" or "art" of magic that occurs when we take what we've learned about the spiritual world and weave this knowledge together with purpose. The witch breathes activity and life into these things through meditation, trance, ritual, and the spoken word—all things that this book will demonstrate for you in the pages that follow.

The incredible amount of knowledge and wisdom that describe these materials and the practices surrounding their use is what I think about when I hear the term *eclectic witchcraft*. In many ways, I think that all witchcraft is eclectic when you get to the bottom of things. No matter where you learned the magical arts or what traditions inspired those arts, the body of knowledge witches and occultists work with is intentionally curated. We explore our surroundings, conditions, and what we have, and we curate our spells and rites accordingly.

As we learn more and gain more experience, we refine our skills by using what works best. This is what we mean when we say that witchcraft is a science. The witch is an explorer, experimenter, and scientist (and yeah, sometimes you'll feel like a mad scientist!). The eclectic nature of witchcraft is crucial to this process. Having the freedom to tap into the vast landscape of magical lore puts you in the best position possible to curate a craft that's as unique as you are. This is why you'll see Charlotte suggesting that you journal on your work and experiences. While we can and should rely on the teachings of those who came before us to build a strong foundation, only you can design a magical strategy that's tailor-made for your own practice.

In *Eclectic Witchcraft* you'll survey a wide array of materials, teachings, and approaches to the magical arts. This might feel like an enormous amount of information at first, and it is! My advice is to work your way through with a sense of excitement, joy, and curiosity. Something I appreciate about Charlotte's approach is that she infuses witchcraft training with an air of fun. While the inner work of witchcraft may have its difficult moments (as all evolutionary work does), the value of joy cannot be understated. You should feel excited and motivated by the work you're doing. If you've ever stood in the quiet dark by yourself and observed the moon rising in some wild place, you know what I'm talking about. There's a sense of mystery and wonder that makes the little hairs on your arms stick up. That makes the butterflies in your belly flutter. That causes you to glance over your shoulder to see what's standing on the edge of the circle. Embrace this and enjoy it.

At the end of this book, you'll learn about the importance of bringing magic into your everyday life. The spectacular thing about witchcraft is that if you do it enough, you'll start to see yourself become the living embodiment of magic.

You become the *materia magica* and the *ars magica*, both the body of magic and its art, all wrapped into one. As we weave our spells, we become what is woven. As we sing our enchantments, we become enchanted. I daresay this is the goal of nearly every witch.

Finally, you'll come to learn that even when you reach the end of this book, even if you absorb and perform all the rites within it, there is always more to study and understand. I am reminded of two of the maxims carved within the Temple of Apollo at Delphi: "know thyself" and "surety brings ruin." The work of the witch is never done, and the most effective witches out there know that continual learning and a healthy relationship with our egos is the recipe for success. In the meantime, there's certainly enough quality teachings here to keep you busy for quite some time!

Happy witching,
David Salisbury

INTRODUCTION

Human beings are wildly complex creatures. We are the sum of not only our experiences but our surroundings, our influences, and our culture. We do not exist inside a vacuum, but rather, we evolve through each of our connections. These encounters with the world build us into multifaceted beings with different interests, ideas, opinions, and tastes. Each of us experiences not only our reality but our spirituality through our own unique lens. So, naturally, the flavor of one practitioner's practice will vary greatly from the next—and there is so much beauty to be found in this.

Oftentimes, witchcraft is a solitary journey. Although this can be a wonderful way to create a spiritual path that resonates with you, the initial stages of the journey can be challenging. I want to be very clear that there is no singular right way to create your own path, but there are plenty of opportunities to expand your base knowledge of the craft, though, and that is what birthed the existence of this book.

My goal in writing the pages of this book is to assist new practitioners in learning about the fundamentals of witchcraft. Whether you read this from cover to cover or simply skip to the parts of interest, I want to provide a solid, fleshed out guide to assist you in your growing practice. I want this book to be kept in your library and returned to over and over as needed.

Keep in mind, the pages of this book are from my own practice, and they're the sum of my own experiences and the knowledge that I've accumulated along the way. I encourage others to take what works for them and to leave the rest.

What I mean by this is that not every aspect of my practice will light a spark of interest for you at the time of reading. Perhaps it never will, and that's for you to decide. A witch isn't defined by their crystal collection or their ability to read tarot. In fact (and full disclosure), these two avenues aren't even inherently witchy in their own right.

Creating your own practice is a lengthy process, and it's one that is fueled by inspiration and intuition. What sparks our interest doesn't apply solely to the initial stages of our journey but also to the building of your practice. It's key to allow yourself to move and flow toward what intrigues you. This is your intuition guiding you. My own practice doesn't look the same as other witches', even to those whom I'm close to, and that's not only acceptable but encouraged. One of the biggest draws of witchcraft is the ability to create a spiritual practice that is unique to you. While I will be guiding you, I will not be limiting you.

If you see a particular spell or exercise and you're short on materials—or perhaps the language simply isn't for you—you have the freedom to substitute and revise as needed. Use the lists of correspondences to craft your own workings. After all, infusing our work with our own intentions and energy is vital.

People are often hesitant to start for fear of making a mistake. Rest assured, mistakes will be made, but they will be the most efficient teachers. Mistakes allow us to access what's working and what needs fine-tuning. Your practice will grow and evolve as you do. Personally, my own practice has heavily evolved over the years, and that's to be expected.

My curiosity about witchcraft peaked when the era of glorious cult classic movies such as *Hocus Pocus* (1993), *The Craft* (1996), and *Practical Magic* (1998) came into being. That said, I consider myself to have been a Pagan for my entire life of conscious thought. I was raised without religion and given the freedom to explore my own at an early age. I was one of the children frolicking in the woods, gathering supplies for my potions and spells. The deep connection we, as humans, have with the earth and the currents of energy surrounding us was something I innately understood.

Naturally I am not the same witch I was in the late 1990s—despite still frolicking in the woods. For starters, I would not currently consider myself to be a Wiccan, but that's the exact place I started. Let me tell you, the boom of occult books today was nothing like it was back in '90s and early aughts. By and large, the vast majority of reading material was Wicca-centric. This was the starting place of my exploration, and if there is anything my current surplus of reading material has shown me, this was not an unusual place for most practitioners of my era to start. While I can't deny the Wiccan influence in portions of my own practice, I am not limited by it.

Much of my practice today is making use of the earth's materials as well as paying heed to lunar cycles. I grow my own herbs in my garden and fight against the Florida sun's rays from frying my babies on a nearly daily basis. Due to these interests, spell jars make a regular appearance in my practice as well as astrology. I am also a candle magick enthusiast who has dressed a candle or two in her day.

Present day, I run a Pagan shop called Eclectic Charge, and its corresponding Instagram page as well, which is where I display my teachings in a creative, visual format. When I'm not writing, fulfilling orders, or creating graphics, I also cohost a delightfully witchy podcast called *Cosmic Cauldron* that airs every Wednesday. And, as to not disappoint those who make use of the spells I share online, I have included a chapter dedicated to my spells plus a guide on how to create your own.

Though there has been a recent increase in the popularity of witchcraft, I am acutely aware of what it is like to not practice aloud. Historically, when my beliefs would come into conversation, I would recite a phrase like "I believe in energy" to whoever was inquiring. I did this particularly when it wasn't someone I felt would respect my views—for whatever reason. While I wasn't lying, I wasn't exactly forthcoming either. The truth is, there are many reasons that people may not be comfortable telling another person that they practice witchcraft, and due to this, each chapter in this book will conclude with "Broom Closet Witch Tips" for those who aren't comfortable practicing in the open yet.

It is my hope in writing this that I give each individual practitioner the tools they will need to develop a practice that works for them. These chapters will serve to help you navigate the initial stages of your journey while you curate a practice that you find personally fulfilling and assist you in deepening your practice and connection to the energy that surround you. I am so incredibly excited to teach in a way that isn't limited by infographics or character caps of social media. Bear with me if I am long-winded. I have had this book in me for a long time, and it has been dying to get out.

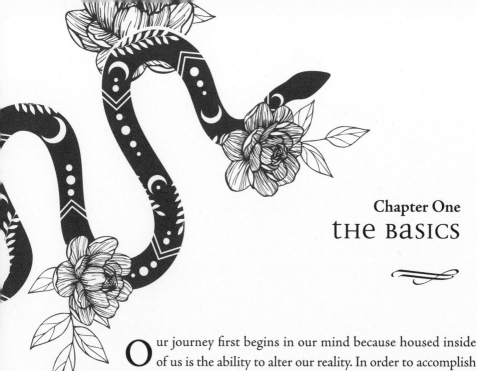

tHe BASICS

O ur journey first begins in our mind because housed inside of us is the ability to alter our reality. In order to accomplish this change, one must first become in tune with themselves. While this may seem daunting or overly complex at first, the process itself is the opposite. In reality, the process involves stepping back from the complexity to invite in the simplicity. Our minds are often like a Grand Central Station of passing thoughts and noises that clutter our focus and impede our ability to be present. It is in this quiet stillness that we become fully aware, not only of our surroundings but of the power we hold within ourselves.

In order to harness our personal power, we must first conquer the mind. This chapter will cover the areas related to the mind while building toward enhancing our power by working with energy. We will focus on understanding the energy inside of us as well as the energy on the outside of us and how we can fuse the two to create powerful manifestations. Sometimes the most powerful spells require zero ingredients and rather rely on clear and precisely directed energy and intention. This chapter will focus on how to accomplish just that.

meDItAtIon

Some would argue that the basics of witchcraft are summed up in tools of the trade. And one would think that, as an occult shop owner, I would enjoy pushing this notion—but I do not. While it might be good for the bottom line, it is against my beliefs.

Multiple studies conducted on the effects of meditation have concluded that powerful changes take place within the minds and bodies of those who participate. Meditation has the ability to help reduce symptoms of anxiety, depression, high blood pressure, pain, and insomnia as well as enhance moods and strengthen our memories.[1] But more so than this, meditation helps to enhance your intuition, increase your self-awareness, and deepen your connection with your higher self.

The most important part of witchcraft is getting your mind in the right place. What I mean by this is that our minds control our very practice. First and foremost, you must be able to harness your mind's powers. You will need to be able to raise energy, ground yourself, channel energy, and otherwise operate on a very cognizant level.

This is no easy feat. It is understandable that people who come to me for beginner's advice groan when I state this is the first step in diving into and expanding their own craft. I get it. As an avid overthinker, quieting the mind and its incessant chatter was one of the biggest hurdles I faced when exploring my own practice. But be that as it may, it was also the most rewarding.

My spellwork became more potent. I had more hits than I had misses—*and yes, there are misses*—my manifestations increased in speed, and my overall well-being improved because I became the master of my own mind. However, this is not a one-and-done type of undertaking. Remaining in tune with yourself and present requires consistency. Whatever that consistency may be for you is of your own choosing, but the more frequent, the better.

Before you start your workings, you need to have an understanding of the basics of meditation and control over your own mind.

If you struggle with either of these, guided meditations are aplenty. Guided meditations are recorded or in-person meditations that are led by a teacher who will coach you into these deep states. The methods the instructors use are varied, and so are the types of guided meditations. Certain guided meditations will have a central focus, such as reducing stress, but oftentimes, their focus is to simply assist you in achieving a meditative state by taking you through the steps sequentially. This type of instruction becomes a gentle reminder to relax your shoulders, loosen your jaw, focus on your breathing, and turn your focus inward, which makes them a great place for those starting out.

---

1. Powell, "When Science Meets Mindfulness," *Harvard Gazette.*

However, I must warn you to give the guided meditation a once-over before you commit to a particular meditation so you can be sure they work for you. I once spent an entire meditation fixated on the fact that someone skipped over a number while counting down. Instead of finding a state of transformation, I desperately needed to know where the number forty-seven had gone. Another time, I was so caught off guard by my vagina being referred to as a "beautiful butterfly" that there was no way for me to recalibrate. These things may be fine for you, or even your cup of tea, but they were passes for me, and why I always like to have an idea of what I am getting into before I commit.

Another meditation tip for quieting your mind is the use of binaural beats. Binaural beats are considered a form of sound wave therapy, and they are best listened to through headphones where each separate frequency can be registered in each individual ear. The basis of this is that by listening to these specific frequencies, your brainwaves start to synchronize to the difference between the two frequencies and will assist you in achieving meditative states of consciousness. Simply listening to these sounds is known to have a similar effect to that of meditation in that it reduces stress, increases focus, and improves memory.[2] Pairing these beats with meditation helps a person achieve a deeper state of meditation by altering their brainwaves and allowing them to focus more intently. Each binaural beat will correspond with a brainwave frequency, and I am including a chart from R. Douglas Fields's *Electric Brain* with the full disclosure that I am not a neuroscientist. Fortunately, he is. Please consult with your doctor if you have a condition such as epilepsy to make sure this is a safe option for you.

Brainwave Frequency Chart

Delta (0.5 to 3 Hz): State of deep sleep and relaxation

These brain waves are most common in deep sleep as well as other states of unconsciousness, such as being under anesthesia or in a coma.

Theta (4 to 7 Hz): REM sleep, meditation, and creative states

These brain waves are most common when we are daydreaming or drifting off to sleep.

---

2. Smith, "What Are Binaural Beats, and How Do They Work?"

Alpha (8 to 13 Hz): Decreases anxiety and promotes positivity

These brain waves are most common when we are in a very relaxed state, such as meditation.

Beta (14 to 30 Hz): Increased focus and concentration

These brain waves are most common when we are busy with a task.

Gamma (30+ Hz): Enhanced cognitive ability

These brain waves are most common when we are very alert and active.[3]

While both binaural beats and guided meditations are great for the preliminary steps in achieving trancelike states, the ultimate goal is to be able to access these states without them—and on demand. That said, we cannot walk before we crawl. You must find comfort within your own mind and your own ability to access these states—assisted or otherwise—before you can truly harness your own power.

It should also be noted that formal meditation itself is not the only way to access trancelike states. In fact, many neurodivergent individuals may struggle with those methods. As there are many ways to induce trancelike states, I encourage individuals to pay attention to when they become lost in a rhythmic wave. This could be during exercise or an activity that brings them into a flow state. One simple method is known as walking meditation. In this method, we are not asking our body to rest alongside our mind. Quite the opposite. Walking meditation is accomplished by focusing on your breathing and the pace of your footsteps as you go for a stroll. The goal here isn't to be walking on autopilot but rather to focus on our actions and be present in the moment. As you walk, feel your breath and your feet connecting with the ground beneath you. This is not the only way to achieve an altered state of consciousness, and as long as you're able to achieve it, you shouldn't worry yourself over how you reach the end goal.

Another common question with meditation is: How will I know? When a person is in a meditative state, they will feel lighter and more at peace. While the individual understands that they have a body, they begin to become aware that they are more than just this body in this one space. There is a quiet awareness of their being and their connection to the world around them with a deep sense

---

3. Fields, *Electric Brain*, 101.

of relaxation or even euphoria. While thoughts can (and do) still occur, the person becomes an objective observer rather than actively invested in them. The goal of meditation is not to create a vacuum where thoughts don't exist. Rather, the goal is to observe how much of our thought process occurs automatically. When a thought occurs, observe the thought and release it.

The longer we allow ourselves to remain in meditative states, the deeper we will go. However, when beginning a meditation practice, it is easiest to start off slowly for a set amount of time. You can start by setting a five-minute timer on your phone, and gradually increase your time in subsequent sessions. When you are finished, note how you feel. Do you feel calmer? Are you more aware? Labeling your results allows you to identify the ways in which your practice is working (or not working) and whether or not you will need to do some fine-tuning.

Finding a method that works for you is a process of trial and error, but make a small amount of time each day to commit to it. As your comfort and ability start to expand, increase the length of time until the practice of switching your brainwaves becomes as easy as switching gears. This will take time, and that is okay. Witchcraft is referred to as a practice—and for good reason. Even seasoned witches are constantly learning. Think of this journey as a marathon rather than a sprint. You have time to figure out your path, but you must first start with the foundations.

VISUALIZATION

Visualization is also a vital component of your practice, which I will continue to discuss in further subsections as they are interconnected, and there are many practices you will use visualization in unison with. For instance, you must visualize the harnessing of energy. You must visualize grounding your energy. You must visualize projecting your energy both into your workings and outwardly into the universe. You must visualize boundaries and sacred spaces.

While a lot of practice is negotiable depending on the practitioner, visualization is a necessity. You must visualize in some capacity. Magick is working with energy. Depending on your practice, this may be solely your own, or you may have assistance with other external energies. But the fact remains: visualization is key.

That said, what that visualization looks like can be as individual as the practitioner. For most of my own workings, my visualizations and manipulation of energies are seen to me as light. Whether I am grounding, raising energy, or casting a shield of protection around me, it is light. This does not have to be the same for you.

While grounding, you can envision roots stemming up from the earth and connecting with the soles of your feet. When drawing energy down from the skies, you can envision a rope pulling down into you. What you are visualizing is not nearly as important as the fact that you *are* visualizing, so you needn't be hung up in someone else's formalities. However the energy that presents itself to you is how you should work with it.

Now, while this subsection is labeled "visualization" and it is emphasized, keep in mind that visualization could present itself differently from one person to the next.

Visualizations don't have to be elaborate to be effective. In fact, they do not have to be seen as visualizations at all. Some individuals may struggle to obtain a vision in any capacity. If this is the case for you, you may find that having a marker in the physical world may enhance your concentration. You can make use of candles or chalk outlines in the setting of your energetic boundary. If you're imbuing an object with energy, you can place the object directly in your hands. The purpose of visualizations, at their core, is to form a connection. When you are in the preliminary stages or even well into the journey, this may be accomplished more easily by making the process more tangible. As you grow into your practice, working with energy eventually becomes palpable. When you reach this point, you will often find yourself less reliant on physicality.

energy work

Once you feel comfortable accessing different states of consciousness and manifesting visualizations, the next step is to practice working with energy. The concept of energy can be difficult to explain, as energy is present everywhere, but per the US Energy Information Administration, energy is often defined as "the ability to do work."[4] In the mundane world, this could be as routine as mustering up the energy to slide into your office chair on Monday morning. But, on the other hand, it can be as exhilarating as directing energy with your intentions and creating a reality that is aligned with your goals.

---

4. "What Is Energy?" US Energy Information Administration.

Raising Energy

What does it mean to raise energy? This concept goes back to everything consisting of energy and magick being the ability to manipulate that energy. Energy is a part of everything, and it originates from two main types of sources: internal and external. Internal sources come from within, whereas external sources are channeled through sources outside of ourselves. Our practices and what they consist of will determine the sources of energies that we tap into and whether we work with deities, crystals, herbs, or any number of other items that each possess their individual energies.

Now, why must we raise energy? Because our internal energy stores are finite and can be depleted. Ever wondered why it is called spell*work*? That is because it *is*. It is work.

In order to make the most out of our workings, we must raise energy or even borrow energy from any of the sources we choose to work with. But our first stop is always within. We must raise our own internal energy to put the most punch in our spells.

We can raise our own energy in a few different ways:

Chanting: The use of "om" or even the rhythmic use of words and phrases can raise energy.

Movement: Any movement that gets the heart pumping drums up energy. There is a little limitation here, and you can use your imagination. But, for input's sake, dancing can be used as well as other forms of cardio. You can also make use of clapping or drumming.

Channeling emotion: Spellwork stems from a desire. Whatever that desire may be, use that emotion to tap into your energy stores and put it into motion.

As stated, you can also pull energy from external sources to assist you with your workings. This allows you access to outside energies where you are not solely reliant on your own. For instance, when we are working with herbs, crystals, or lunar cycles, we are also tapping into their energy to enhance our workings. If working with deities is a part of your practice, you can also ask them to lend their energy to your workings. There is an abundance of outside energy that can be utilized in your practice, and each individual must explore what they're most drawn to as well as what works for them.

How much energy is needed? That answer requires us to look at the type of magick we are performing. At times, simple ingredients and intention will suffice, and you may not need to call in reinforcements. You may be just fine using the tools at your disposal. Not all workings require an absorbent amount of energy. Trust your judgment when it comes to how much energy you will need to achieve your own goal. You can always try again if you miss the mark, so don't be afraid of making mistakes as they are the best teachers.

Directing Energy

The ability to direct energy is as important as the ability to raise it. Once we have built up our energy, we must direct it. While there are tools, such as the athame or wand, that can be used to direct energy for practices such as casting a circle or channeling it into an object or symbol, they are not necessary. Our hands and fingers can tackle the job just as well.

In some practices, such as Wicca, practitioners raise and direct energy in a method referred to as the "cone of power." The title itself is a reference to the form the energy takes shape. Creating a cone of power is often practiced in groups but can be done alone. When the energy is called down by the group or solitary practitioner, it takes the shape of a cone with the circumference taking the shape of a circle surrounding the practitioners. The energy is directed through the cone's point.

Directing energy is paired with visualization, as you will need to visualize the energy flowing from yourself into an object, outward into the universe, or into an energetic boundary, such as a circle. This is a skill that is developed over time. The more often we practice working with energy and directing it, the more proficient we will become. A common method of visualization is to envision building an orb of light in the palms of your hands. As you practice, the energy will begin to feel more tangible, and you will be able to understand that you are progressing. You will then be able to focus your intention on transferring the energy into an item, such as a crystal. Once this is complete, you may pick the item up. If you can feel the energetic difference of the item, your task has been successfully completed.

GROUNDING

After raising energy, you may find that you have accumulated a surplus, which may manifest as tingling or other stimuli. That remaining energy needs to go somewhere, which is where grounding comes in. Grounding is taking that residual energy we raised prior to and during our spellwork and transmuting it elsewhere. What goes up must come down—lest we be running around like we have had an IV drip of pure espresso. No need for that.

The energy that was raised can be transmuted in a few different ways. Of these ways, a number of them require visualization to direct that energy outward and away from us.

+ First, we can take the term *grounding* quite literally and send the energy outward, back into the earth. Admittedly, this is my favorite tried-and-true method.

+ You can also transfer the excess energy into an object, such as a crystal or a body of water, that can absorb it.

+ Eat up! Ideally, you would consume earthy foods to ground you. The energy will then be consumed by breaking down and processing the foods to nourish you.

As we have touched on before, not all spellwork will require an extensive amount of raised energy. While grounding won't be necessary in every situation, it is good to practice it for spells that require more energy. However, it is best to start out small in the beginning and gradually increase the intensity of your spells.

The methods covered in this chapter are necessary steps in building your practice. After all, before we can get to the meat of witchcraft, we must begin to understand the bare bones. We need to have knowledge about the framework of our practice, and the concepts we have covered in this chapter are fundamental to every facet of witchcraft. These "bare bones" are the concepts you will first need to set your sights on in order to make changes in the world around you. Remember: as above, so below. You must first be able to make changes within yourself before you are able to influence change in the world around you.

Witchcraft in Action
eneRCy woRk pRactice

The key to expanding our abilities is to practice. The following exercise is one such method that you can put into action to assist you with both visualization and working with energy.

Directions:

1. Allow yourself some quiet time and get into a state of relaxation.

2. Visualize the energy around you.

3. Place your palms approximately two to three inches apart and feel the sensation on your hands. That's energy. Move your palms toward and away from each other as the energy builds. Cup your hands around the energy as you shape it and compress it.

4. While doing step 3, set an intention for this orb in your mind, and hold it there as you focus on channeling your intention into the orb. Feel the edges of the energy. Can you feel the currents more powerfully, or have they changed in some way? If not, try the exercise once more. Compact the energy further and keep your intention at the forefront of your mind as you focus on channeling it outwards.

5. Once you have identified the energetic change, release this orb of intention upward into the universe.

6. If there is any residual energy, go outside and ground the energy in the earth by placing your hands directly on the ground.

Broom Closet Witch Tips

. . . .

The wonderful thing about meditation and working with energy is that it does not require a single tool. It's easy to conceal our practice when we are the only thing we need to accomplish the task. There are no tarot cards or altar supplies or strange bones to put away before the company arrives. This makes meditation, energy work, and visualization a great starting place. It's cost-effective, *and* it doesn't leave behind any trace of evidence.

Practices such as meditation can take place in private spaces or even in public in the form of group meditations. You may also find practices like yoga to be highly meditative as well, particularly if being still during seated meditation is difficult. As meditation itself is an ancient practice, you will not alert anyone to your beliefs by practicing meditation. If questioned, you can always default to a response about how you are trying to practice mindfulness. Besides, it *is* true.

For practices such as grounding, you can make use of your own backyard or parks nearby. If those are not options, houseplants make a great way to bring the outdoors indoors. Using houseplants is also a great practice if you are living in a crowded city or simply don't feel like explaining yourself to your neighbors. Bonus, plants are wonderful energetic purifiers for our spaces and are known to reduce stress and sharpen our focus.[5] Be mindful of what types of plants you bring into your home if you have curious children or pets, though, because many common indoor plants are poisonous to both.

---

5. Stanborough, "A Hobby for All Seasons."

Chapter Two
PROTECTION magick

P rotection magick is arguably the single most important magick you should put into place at the beginning of your practice. You must protect your sacred spaces, your home, and your person. When we dive into the spiritual world, we are tapping into energies. Some are well beyond our understanding, particularly in the initial stages of learning, and the best defense is a good offense.

As we explore our paths, we practice developing sensitivities to the energies around us. As we enhance these sensitivities, we become more susceptible. This is sometimes described as us emitting a beacon into the spiritual and energetic realm that alerts energies to our presence—both good and bad. While allowing ourselves to develop our skills is necessary, this can leave us vulnerable to accepting energies that don't belong to us or, worse, energies that have been targeted against us. We must protect ourselves from not only malicious or negative spirits and energies but people as well.

While there are many practices for preventing and removing such energies, I will present what works best for me. Protections can come in many forms, and there is no one-size-fits-all method. In fact, many choose to have more than one system in place, which is a strategy that I encourage.

WARDS

One form of protection magick that falls under the category of preventive is the use of wards. The word *ward* itself means to "guard" or "watch over." And that is exactly the purpose here. Wards are used to create an energetic barrier. While wards are generally created as a long-term protection method, they can also be temporary and take on many forms. They can be any number of items, and some of these items include amulets, talismans, charms, and even spell jars. Wards can be worn to protect you or placed strategically around your home to protect your property and place of practice. Some popular home protection wards include bells and horseshoes, but do not let this stop you. This is your craft, remember? If you have an item that resonates with you, choose this item and imbue it with the energy of protection.

The next question is: Where should you place your item? Naturally, this is going to depend on the size of the item and the spatial capacity. Want to keep negative energies at bay from entering your home? Place a ward over or around your front door to keep unwanted energies from passing your threshold. If the item is small enough, you can keep the ward on your person. I like to refer to this as on-the-go protection.

My personal practice makes use of spell jars, which can vary in size, and the smallest of these I like to craft into necklaces. These spell jars combine the properties of crystals as well as the properties of herbs and even oils and other items to create an efficient ward that can be worn for personal protection. Of course, spell jars can be used for many purposes, and I will be digging further into the topic in chapter 10.

BANISHING

Related to the use of wards, banishing is a practice that borders on preventive, particularly if it is performed daily. Banishing can be accomplished in a few different ways, and it's most effective when it's done on a consistent basis. Banishing works to clear stagnant energies as well as negative energies that have accumulated in your space. These energies can be brought in by other people, spirits, or malcontent. The best thing you can do for yourself and your space is to clear the energy thoroughly and often.

One of the most popular methods of clearing energy is smoke cleansing. If you have some older books about witchcraft on your shelf, you may have heard this coined as "smudging." While the word itself is English in origin, the term is often used to describe a ceremony sacred to Indigenous people. The practice is considered closed to those who are not of this community and makes use of white sage, or *Salvia apiana*. The use of this herb outside of Indigenous groups has grown rapidly, and this rise in popularity has raised concerns about overharvesting and sustainability.[6] While white sage is a wonderful herb, there are so many other options to choose from.

Some replacement herb bundles for white sage include garden sage, rosemary, juniper, bay leaf, and lavender. Keep in mind that this is not an exhaustive list. There are so many herbs that you can utilize to cleanse your space. In my practice, I cleanse myself with the smoke first, and then I work throughout my home, paying special attention to entryways and windows. If the energy is particularly irksome, I open the doors and windows and usher the energies out with hand gestures as well as audibly requesting that the presence remove itself. I am not a very poetic person, so what this typically looks like for me is saying, "Get out!" whereas another person may be able to construct a more elegant request. However, if it gets the job done, that's fine because that's what counts. In the place of herb bundles, you can also substitute incense in its many forms, using sticks, cones, or even loose incense blends.

Witchcraft in Action
BANISHING INCENSE BLEND

If you are not familiar with loose incense blends, it might surprise you to know that they are super easy to create on your own. There are just a handful of materials, such as a firesafe dish and a mortar and pestle, that you will need to gather, and the following directions will tell you how to mix and use the incense.

While you can typically place charcoal directly in most firesafe containers, you could also add a layer of salt at the bottom to protect your dish from the heat and utilize the protective energies of salt.

---

6. Leopold, "What Is Going On with White Sage?"

Materials:
* ½ teaspoon dried basil (for protection)
* ½ teaspoon dried rosemary (to ward off negativity)
* ½ teaspoon dried lavender (to cleanse space)
* ½ teaspoon dried chamomile (to promote peace and healing)
* Mortar and pestle
* Small airtight jar
* Salt, optional
* Firesafe dish, such as a small cauldron or cast-iron dish
* Charcoal disc
* Tongs
* Lighter

Directions:
1. Combine the herbs in the mortar.
2. Grind your ingredients with the pestle, focusing on the intention of banishing.

    Note: The mixture doesn't need to be a powder consistency, but you do need to break down any of the larger pieces for easier burning.
3. Place the herb mixture in an airtight jar, and set it off to the side.
4. If desired, prepare your firesafe container by placing a layer of salt on the bottom.
5. Holding the charcoal with the tongs, use the lighter to light the charcoal on fire. Allow five to ten minutes for the charcoal to heat up to temperature. You will notice a layer of ash forming on the top of the charcoal when it's ready.
6. Place the charcoal in a firesafe dish.
7. Grab a pinch of the incense mix and place it directly on the charcoal.
8. Envision the incense smoke clearing out the unwanted energies. Allow the mix to burn fully. If you would like to add more of the mixture to the charcoal, feel free to do so.
9. Keep any remaining incense in the airtight jar for later use.

Witchcraft in Action
BANISHING SPRAY

This is my own recipe for a banishing spray with steps for how to use it. This recipe uses ever-so-handy witch's black salt, and you can find directions for how to make it at the end of this section.

Materials:
* 1 cup water
* 1-quart saucepan
* Mixing spoon
* Strainer
* Large bowl
* 1 small spray bottle
* ½ teaspoon witch's black salt
* 1 teaspoon dried rosemary (for protection)
* 1 teaspoon dried garden sage (for cleansing)

Directions:
1. Place the water in the saucepan and bring the water to a boil.
2. Once the water is boiling, add the herbs and witch's black salt.
3. Use the spoon to stir the mixture counterclockwise for banishing.
4. Once the water has slightly yellowed, remove the saucepan from the heat. Strain the water into the bowl, disposing of the herbs.
5. Once the mixture has cooled, pour it into the spray bottle.
6. Thoroughly spray the mixture around your home, paying particular attention to entryways.
7. Store this spray in your refrigerator to prolong use. While the use of dried herbs extends its shelf life, it's best to use the spray within a couple of weeks of its creation.

Witchcraft in Action
WITCH'S BLACK SALT

Witch's black salt can be incorporated into many other recipes and spells. It can also be used for banishing all by itself.

Materials:
* 2 tablespoons sea salt
* 1 tablespoon smoke cleansing or incense ashes
* 2 ground eggshells, optional
* Mortar and pestle
* Small airtight jar

Directions:
1. Combine all the ingredients in the mortar.
2. Use the pestle to grind the ingredients until you produce a fine powderlike consistency.
3. Sprinkle small pinches of the salt around the entryways in your house.
4. Keep any remaining powder in the airtight jar.

REVERSALS

Often—and by "often," I mean several times a week—I am contacted by someone who believes that they have been cursed, hexed, or otherwise jinxed. While I like to implore people to consider the mundane before the magickal, the truth of the matter is that it is not impossible, particularly given how widespread the occult has become in recent years. It is not unheard of for dabblers to be interested in a cosmic justice of sorts. Who has not wanted to be the judge, jury, and executioner when they have been wronged or suffered a perceived slight?

All of that—coupled with the hex-positive attitudes that have been ushered in—means the likelihood that a person could be the unfortunate recipient of a magickal assault is ever increasing. That said, I must clarify that this hex-positive shift is not without its benefits, and if the situation is warranted, I have no ill regard for this practice.

My views aside, let us get back to the matter at hand. You have been cursed. Now what? My preferred method is to stack the practices previously included with a few other methods that I will cover here. Breaking a curse, hex, or jinx takes a lot of elbow grease. Figuratively speaking, of course, though I am sure if you scoured the internet, you would be able to find a spell that requires just that.

Some of the common methods used to break curses that I will be going over in detail include:

+ Unbinding spells
+ Mirror spells
+ Herbal and salt baths
+ Reverse candles
+ Poppet dolls

HERBAL AND SALT BATHS

My first recommendation for breaking curses is to perform a ritual bath. I follow the order of a ritual bath as the first step, and I do it before combining another method. These baths can be used independently from hex breaking, and they can be quite glorious as a stand-alone ritual in your practice.

There are several different herbs and types of salt that can be used for hex breaking, and while the ritual bath I've included calls for specific ingredients, you can work off the following lists to create your own baths and other spells.

Herbs for Hex Breaking

Angelica: Exorcism, healing, and protection

Cinquefoil: Money, protection, and sleep

Garlic: Exorcism, healing, and protection

Gentian: Hex-breaking and power

Ginseng: Curse removal, healing, and protection

Huckleberry: Hex-breaking and protection

Hyssop: Protection and purification

Lime: Healing and protection

Thistle: Hex-breaking, protection, and strength

Vetiver: Hex-breaking and luck

Wintergreen: Healing, hex-breaking, and protection

Salts for Hex Breaking

Black lava salt: This salt is used for protection, absorbing and dispelling negative energy, and purification.

Common salt: In a pinch, table salt will do. As a salt, it carries with it the properties of protection and purification.

Dead Sea salt: Dead Sea salt is not composed of sodium chloride like other salts, but this salt is useful for banishing and protection.

Epsom salt: Much like Dead Sea salt, this is not the same mineral composition as other salts, but it is still a wonderful addition to include in any ritual bath. It is used for curse-breaking, purification, and dispelling negative energies.

Witch's black salt: This is my favorite salt to use in protection magick and banishing rituals. As shown in my recipe, this salt is made by grinding sea salt and ashes from smoke cleansing or incense burning. Some practitioners like to add ground eggshells for an additional layer of protection.

Witchcraft in Action
Hex-Breaking Bath

This is a ritual bath I have designed for both cleansing and breaking curses. The candles used in it can be of any size.

Materials:
* Rosemary smoke-cleansing bundle
* Lighter or matches
* 1 to 2 pieces of tourmaline (for protection)
* 1 to 2 pieces of clear quartz (to amplify intention)
* Black candles (for protection)

* 1 cup Epsom salt (for hex-breaking)
* 2 whole lemons cut in half (for hex-breaking)

Directions:

1. Before running your bath water, cleanse the area as well as yourself with the herb bundle. To do this, begin by lighting your herb bundle and tracing the perimeters of your physical body with the intention of ridding yourself of the unwanted energy. Once you've extinguished the bundle, cleanse the tub and surrounding area.

2. Place the quartz around the tub as the stone is generally considered water safe.

3. Place the tourmaline near the tub but far enough away from the water so it won't be damaged.

4. Start to fill your tub with water. As it fills, pour the Epsom salt into the tub.

5. Squeeze the juice of each lemon half into the bath water.

6. Place your candles around the bath, making sure you are not creating a fire hazard, and light them.

7. Soak in your bath while focusing on the power of the hex, curse, or jinx being lifted. Cleanse yourself thoroughly with the water, using it to wash the energy away.

8. When you are done, you can simply send the water down the drain and extinguish the candles.

MIRROR SPELLS

Mirrors have a magickal presence in and of themselves. From fairy tales to folktales, there has been an allure surrounding mirrors for centuries—and with good reason. Whether used for scrying or repelling negative energy, a simple mirror can be a powerful tool in your arsenal.

Witchcraft in Action
MIRROR SPELL

To start this spell, you will need a mirror. Some practitioners specify that the mirror needs to be small and round, but in my experience, size and shape are not as important as assigning the mirror its task. I perform this spell with the wall mirror around my home. However, there is nothing wrong with using a traditional small, round mirror, and a compact mirror would be excellent for such an occasion.

Materials:
*   Mirror
*   2 black chime or birthday candles
*   Lighter or matches

Directions:
1. Place the candles safely near the mirror, making sure they're in your vision.
2. Light your candles and hold your intention of removing the negative energy in your mind for the duration of the spell.
3. Focus on the mirror, and see it becoming not only a shield for you but also a springboard to repel and return any magickal malice that has been placed upon you.
4. As the candle burns, recite:

    From my space, you must retreat.
    Return to sender. So mote it be.

5. If using a mirror that you can move, place it in a window or near an entryway, and allow the candles to burn down. Using chime or birthday candles will expedite this process. However, you can snuff out the candles when necessary.

poppet dolls

While poppet dolls are a staple in occultism, they are not the first item I grab when I have work to do, but I will not shortchange their effectiveness. If poppet dolls are of interest to you, there are a few ways they can be used to redirect and remove curses. First, you will need a doll. You can get as crafty or as simple as you want. If you are not one for crafts, a Barbie or similar doll will do the trick. If you know, for a fact, the person who has hexed you, you can create or purchase a doll in their likeness. I recommend you be absolutely certain about who hexed you before going this route.

If this is a preventive measure and the curse has not taken place, one route is to create a poppet doll in the potential offender's honor. After assembling the doll, you would bind the doll with a cord while reciting words that state the person is incapable of committing harm against you. Of course, binding them from performing magick against you is only the way to go if the curse is not already in action. Alas, if the curse has already taken place, this is not going to be of much assistance.

What you can do instead is create a poppet doll of your own likeness. Much like imbuing the mirror with intention in the previous spell, you will need to assign this poppet doll its purpose. And the purpose of this poor doll is to take the hit of the curse on your behalf. Better it than you!

Once you feel that the damage is over, dispose of this doll. Try to remember to be as environmentally friendly as possible in doing so. You also want this doll as far away from you as possible. If the materials are not hazardous, a good way to dispose of a poppet is to burn the doll in a firepit. If the materials are biodegradable, you could also bury the doll. As a last resort, depending on the materials used, you should dispose of the doll in the garbage bin.

reversal candles

Have you seen those dual-colored candles in Pagan shops? Typically, the top will be white or red and the bottom black. These candles can be used to reverse and send back the curse or hex to whoever laid it upon you in the first place. Candle magick is an old, simple practice, but it can be as decadent and ceremonial as you would like. The key here is to build energy and channel it. The act of lighting the candle and watching the flame can be trancelike in nature, which allows you to access the state of mind you need to be in when performing magick—particularly of this nature.

The black portion of the candle is representative of the curse, whereas the lighter portion represents overcoming said curse or sending it back to its originator. This, again, is dependent on your intention, as you're the one performing the spellwork. If you know who sent the energy, their name can be carved in the bottom with your name etched at the top. Afterward, simply light the candle and focus on the spell being broken as it burns down.

UNBINDING SPELLS

Unbinding spells are not exclusive to the corner of magick that occupies the hexing and cursing arena. On the contrary, these spells are often used in place of cutting cords and ties with people and energies you no longer align with. That said, they are also effective at "unbinding" a maleficent spell on account of them being symbolic of undoing something—be it a person, bad habit, or a curse.

Witchcraft in Action
UNBINDING SPELL

Much like binding spells, you are going to need a cord to perform this magick. Some traditions are stringent on what color and material this should be, but in my practice, the symbolism works the same regardless. More often than not, I like to be resourceful by using what I have on hand. You will also need two candles and a surface that is fire-resistant, such as concrete, to perform this safely. If using a fire-resistant surface is not an option, you can place the candles in a long dish, such as a baking pan, with a layer of salt at the bottom.

Materials:
  * 2 chime candles (black or white) with chime candle holders
  * 1 foot string
  * Lighter or matches
  * Fire-resistant surface

Directions:

1. Form a knotted loop in each end of your string.

2. Place your chime candles into holders approximately six inches apart.

3. Place a loop around each of the candles and position your candles to ensure the string is snug. The knot placement should be toward the upper-middle portion of each candle.

4. Light both candles.

5. Focus your intention on separating yourself from the curse and channel it into the candles.

6. As the candles burn, the string will catch fire. This is symbolic of the separation between you and the curse.

7. Continue to keep the outcome you desire in your mind's eye as you watch the candles burn down. Do not, for any reason, leave these candles unattended.

8. Once the candles have burned down, dispose of the wax and ashes.

Broom Closet Witch Tips

Protection methods that are placed energetically are, by their nature, extremely easy to conceal. If you are not open with your practice, this is a method that you can easily use without detection. However, most wards are nondescript by themselves. Take the horseshoe, for example. This shape is considered a common symbol of luck and good fortune. While it is most definitely a superstitious practice, it's widespread. This symbol can be placed in your room or worn as jewelry without raising too many questions about the symbolism of the item itself.

With the self-care movement going strong, luxurious baths are far from uncommon. Baths are also typically of a private nature, and Epsom salt is a common item added to baths. If you find yourself in need of a cleansing ritual bath, you should be able to do so undetected. Some of the common hex-breaking herbs are obscure, but lime juice can be used in their place.

While a poppet doll is a conspicuous item, a Barbie or other common doll isn't. Of course, depending on your age range, you're likely to encounter a few raised eyebrows. If you're quick on your feet or this isn't a concern of yours, this may be a viable option. You should take this into consideration when deciding whether this is a method you would like to utilize.

Chapter Three
WHeeL of THe YeaR

as a person moves forward on their path, they develop not only a deeper connection with themselves but with the world around them. They begin to notice what phase the moon is in or the trees shedding their leaves through an entirely new lens—the lens of a witch, of course. They become aware that time is no longer solely linear but cyclical as well, which is evident from the sun moving slowly from its northernmost point to its southernmost point throughout the year, only to cycle back once again.

The Wheel of the Year is a term used to describe the cycling seasons, and it consists of celebrations that take place approximately six weeks from each other throughout the calendar year.

While the Wheel of the Year as we know it today didn't become popularized until the 1950s and 1960s with the Wicca movement, it does have historical ties, and I will be going over its origins as well as the individual festivals, which are referred to as sabbats.

The word *sabbat* is thought to be derived from the word *sabbath* meaning "to rest."[7] In some traditions, magick is to be avoided during the day of these sabbats.[8] This is not my own tradition, but it is something to consider. Personally, I enjoy working with the energy these days provide.

---

7. Mankey, *Witch's Wheel of the Year*, 30.
8. Buckland, *Buckland's Complete Book of Witchcraft*, 97.

Due to the tilt of the axis of the earth, during half of the year, one hemisphere is tilted away from the sun, while the other is tilted toward it. With this in mind, I will be listing Northern and Southern Hemisphere dates for these sabbats. As you read on, you will find that both a feast and decorated altar are central themes.

An altar is a sacred space that can be used as a workspace or a place of worship. The altar itself can be created by using any space available to you, which could include a table, a bookshelf, a chest, or anywhere with enough surface space to include your tools, offerings, and honoring for the seasons. Each section will conclude with a list of items that correspond with the sabbat, which you can place on your altar.

These sabbats are broken down into lesser sabbats and greater sabbats. The lesser sabbats are those that fall on equinoxes and solstices: Ostara, Litha, Mabon, and Yule. The dates of these sabbats will vary from year to year to align with the precise events. For the greater sabbats, or cross-quarter days, you have Imbolc, Beltane, Lammas, and Samhain. These holidays fall in between the solstices and the equinoxes and occur on set dates every year. They are considered the high holidays because they occur at the midpoint, or peak, between the two. Due to this, their energy is more palpable.

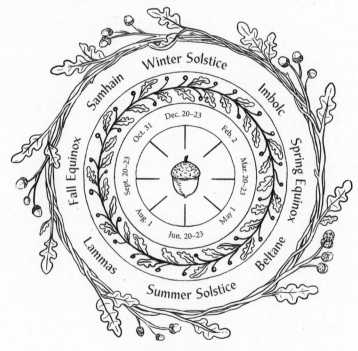

Wheel of the Year

While some of the sabbats are rooted in historical celebrations, others have less clear historical context. Most frequently, though, the sabbats are considered Celtic in origin as there is evidence of these celebrations occurring around the same time. Some are also thought to have Germanic, Greek, and Roman influences as well.[9] However, it is unlikely that today's Wheel of the Year was based solely on these traditions, and whether we use the Wheel of the Year in our own practice—and how we use it—is entirely up to us.

That said, Paganism is an earth-based religion, and there's merit in the cause for celebration. The Wheel of the Year is an excellent way to honor nature and the seasons and growth, death, and rebirth.

If you do not connect with a particular sabbat, do not feel obligated to participate. Perhaps there's something in your own familial tradition or culture that you can blend in place of the sabbats that you feel more connected to. It could be Día de los Muertos, Hanukkah, Kwanzaa, Juneteenth, Veterans Day, Christmas, or any other holiday. What the holiday is does not matter as much as its importance to you and that it aligns with who you are.

We are not here to fit into boxes, and there are no hard and fast rules for following these sabbats. Carving out your own path should be as individual to you as your personality, your interests, your history, your likes, and your dislikes. Witchcraft is not an organized religion, and you will not find a list of commandments damning you if you don't practice a certain way.

But for the sake of this chapter, let us review these sabbats, and you can decide which ones to keep, which ones to toss, and which ones to personalize or replace.

samhain

Northern Hemisphere: October 31
Southern Hemisphere: May 31

Samhain, pronounced SAH-win, is a Gaelic word that translates to "summer's end," as this day was representative of the beginning of the dark half of the year. This is one of the four quarterly Pagan fire festivals, and it is Celtic in origin. As a Celtic fire festival, a bonfire was lit. Participants are thought to have worn animal masks, and sacrifices—crops or livestock—were placed in the fire to ensure the community's

---

9. Mark, "Wheel of the Year."

survival throughout the winter. Before returning home, members would take a flame from the communal fire to light their hearth. While documents on the exact historical festivities can be sparse, this was believed to be a time when the veil was thinning, and themes of communing with the dead and divination were prevalent.[10]

With the spread of Christianity, it is proposed that the Catholic Church thought it would be easier to convert people by incorporating existing holidays into their calendar, and as such, All Saints' Day was created. Originally this took place in May, but it was later moved to November 1, and it maintained some of the traditions of Samhain.[11] It's speculated that this was due to the Celts' reluctance to not participate in Samhain. The night before All Saints' Day was referred to as All Hallows' Eve, and this became the initial emergence of Halloween that we know today.

For many Wiccans and Pagans, Samhain represents the New Year, and this is likely due to this date being considered the Celtic New Year. Many of the sabbats that we are familiar with today have Celtic origins, at least in part, but the official Pagan "New Year" is entirely dependent on traditions and beliefs.

The Samhain celebration is one of the original cross-quarter sabbats and, as such, is considered a greater sabbat. As Samhain is celebrated in the liminal space between the Autumn Equinox and the Winter Solstice, the energy is considered most potent, and the celebration today is also known as a time for remembering ancestors and celebrating the accomplishments and harvest of the year. The focus of this sabbat is typically on the cycle of life, death, and rebirth, and it is still considered a time when "the veil between worlds is at its thinnest."[12] With this in mind, offerings can be left out for ancestors and spirits.

There are many ways to participate in this sabbat, and they depend on your own spiritual path and practice. Naturally one way to honor this sabbat is by decorating your altar for the occasion. Another way is to plan ceremonies that celebrate the harvest. Focus on preparing meals with harvested fruits and vegetables, such as squash and pumpkins. Many consider the dinner table a sacred space, so decorate your table in the corresponding decor and prepare your harvest feast.

This is also a time when many Wiccans and Pagans do magick that focuses on the spirit world. Because this sabbat is focused on life and death, it is a good

---

10. History.com Editors, "Samhain."
11. Rajchel, *Samhain*, 18.
12. History.com Editors, "Samhain."

time to work on communicating with ancestors and spirits. This also makes this a great time to focus on divination. We will touch on methods of divination more thoroughly in chapter 12, but you could use a scrying mirror, hold a séance, use a spirit board or talking board, or perform many other types of divination during this time. If Samhain is symbolic of the New Year in your practice, you can use this time to seek guidance for the upcoming year. If your focus is more on the potent energy of this season, you can utilize the energy not only in your divination practice but in your spellwork as well.

Samhain Altar Decorations
+ Dark altar cloths
+ Skulls and skeletons
+ Offerings to your ancestors
+ Darker colored candles as well as oranges and reds
+ Bread
+ Cups of cider, wine, or mead
+ Fallen foliage, such as acorns and leaves

yuLe
Northern Hemisphere: December 21 to 22
Southern Hemisphere: June 20 to 21

Yule, pronounced YOOL, takes place in December in the Northern Hemisphere, and it is the shortest day of the year. This is a lesser sabbat, as it occurs on the Winter Solstice, but this is one of the more popular sabbats next to Samhain. This is likely because several cultures and religions have celebrations near the time of the Winter Solstice. It is a time when much of the world is celebrating, whether it be Hanukkah, Christmas, Kwanzaa, or Yule, and that carries its own magick.

Yule has clear historical ties; the Norse people celebrated Jul, the Romans celebrated Saturnalia, and the ancient Egyptians celebrated the rebirth of Ra.[13] Saturnalia is considered to be one of the most influential celebrations in the shaping of what we know as Yule today. It started as a one-day celebration but later became a

---

13. Wigington, "History of Yule."

weeklong festival that was celebrated between December 17 and 23.[14] This was a period in Roman history where work and schooling would come to a close and celebration would commence. Even enslaved people were given this time to rejoice. They would decorate their doors and homes with wreaths and greenery, and they would feast, dance, gamble, and otherwise celebrate this joyous time of debauchery.[15]

A popular folklore, primarily for Wiccans, during this sabbat is one of Celtic origins. This is the tale of the Oak King, who represents light, and the Holly King, who represents dark. The two kings engage in a battle over who reigns supreme on both the Summer Solstice and Winter Solstice. On Yule, the Oak King wins. This holds true until Litha, the longest day of the year, when they battle once again.[16]

This sabbat can be celebrated in several ways. As with any Pagan sabbat, you can be sure that there will be a feast involved. Celebrate this time with your family and loved ones by hosting a meal, baking your favorite holiday treats, and indulging. Another common practice is to decorate a Yule log, which is essentially a large log to be burned. Each tree has its own correspondences, some of which you can learn about in chapter 5, so you can choose a log that aligns with your future desires. Decorating a Yule log is done by adding greenery, pine cones, berries, and ribbons, as well as candles to the top. When the eve of this sabbat arrives, the Yule log is burned to ensure a prosperous New Year. This tradition is Norse in origin, but like much of history, you can find that it was also reproduced in some capacity in Christianity.

Yule Altar Decorations

+ Holly leaves
+ Gold, red, and green candles
+ Yule log
+ Assorted nuts
+ Dried orange slices
+ Decorative snowflakes or snow
+ Bells
+ Mistletoe

---

14. Pesznecker, *Yule*, 28.
15. History.com Editors, "Saturnalia."
16. History.com Editors, "Winter Solstice."

IMBOLC

Northern Hemisphere: February 1

Southern Hemisphere: August 1

Imbolc, pronounced IM-blk, is a celebration that is meant to welcome the spring and has themes of rebirth, as the earth is beginning to awaken once again. This is a cross-quarter day and is the celebration to mark the halfway point between the Winter Solstice and the Spring Equinox. This was a time when winter food stores would have been close to exhausted, and the success of new crops would be paramount. As such, fertility plays a large role in the honoring of this festival. The first mention of these celebrations was recorded in the tenth century in Irish literature, and it is thought the festival first originated in the British Isles.[17]

Historically, this sabbat was centered around the goddess Brigid. Brigid, who rules the house and hearth, is a goddess of many talents in several different traditions. She is also said to be a goddess of smithcraft, which some practitioners choose to symbolize with hammers and anvils. One of the pre-Christian celebrations included dressing and crafting a doll of Brigid out of oats and stemlike leaves the night before February 1. This tradition carried on and was adapted into a tradition of soaking the doll in water and placing candles around it to dry. This became a part of the Christian celebration that we know today as Candlemas. Brigid was even adapted in Christianity as Saint Brigid, the patron saint of nuns, midwives, and dairymaids.[18]

In modern times, Wiccan and Pagan celebrations can still honor the Irish goddess Brigid, and feminine energy and honoring the goddess can be a fundamental part of this sabbat, but this is not the only way to celebrate. With the timing of Imbolc and its proximity to Valentine's Day, some practitioners choose to incorporate goddesses who represent love from several different pantheons. In other traditions, Brigid has a connection to fairies and is referred to as a sister of the fae. If fae are a part of your practice, this would be a good time to honor them with offerings and representations on your altar.

Many choose to decorate their altar for this occasion in a variety of ways. Typically, there are objects that symbolize the changing of the season, so regional

---

17. History.com editors, "Imbolc."
18. Neal, *Imbolc*, 27.

flowers will make their appearance on some altars. Cauldrons and chalices are also placed on altars to tie in the feminine aspect of the sabbat as well as the water and healing aspects. The altar is also a lovely place to showcase a handcrafted honoring for Brigid, such as a Brigid's cross, which is a woven cross typically made of straw. Due to Brigid's connection with Celtic lore, Celtic symbols pair nicely as well.

Imbolc Altar Decorations

- Red and white candles
- Celtic symbols
- Brigid's cross
- Corn doll
- Spring flowers
- Cauldrons and chalices
- Tributes to goddesses
- Images of fae
- Small hammer or anvils

ostara

Northern Hemisphere: March 19 to 21
Southern Hemisphere: September 20 to 23

Ostara, pronounced ow-STAA-ruh, is one of the lesser sabbats and is celebrated on the Spring Equinox. The name *Ostara* originated from the Germanic goddess Eostre, who is the goddess of dawn.[19] However, this sabbat wasn't officially named until the 1970s when Aidan Kelly, a witch and the founder of the New Reformed Orthodox Order of the Golden Dawn, created a witchcraft calendar. When doing so, he created names for the equinoxes and solstices.[20]

The exact origins of this sabbat can be hard to pinpoint. Not much is known about the historical celebrations that occurred in ancient civilizations. However, this is a time that has themes of resurrection, and this is not only due to

---

19. Connor, *Ostara*, 17.
20. Kelly, "About Naming Ostara, Litha, and Mabon."

the reemergence of spring but due to stories occurring throughout several different pantheons. For example, in Egyptian mythology, there is the resurrection of the god Osiris, who is associated with fertility and vegetation; and in Greek mythology, there is the resurrection of Dionysus, who was a deity associated with spring.[21] It is said that the feast of Eostre, which occurred on the Spring Equinox, was merged with the holiday Easter or, if you are a witch, Ostara.

The Spring Equinox is a natural time on earth when the cold weather of various regions is subsiding and new growth is forming. Spring flowers start to bloom, and the world becomes ripe with fertility. As such, this sabbat's focus is on just that—fertility—with or without the worship of the goddess Eostre. For Ostara, rabbits and hares are considered sacred as symbols of abundant fertility. Insert every connotation you hold to the fornicating of rabbits here. Eggs are also symbolic for they are representations of rebirth and renewal.

This is a time to spend planting the seeds of beginning—both figuratively and literally. If you are a Green Witch or enjoy gardening, and the last freeze has passed, planting a garden would be a wonderful way to commemorate this occasion. Even if you do not enjoy gardening, getting out in nature to appreciate the new growth firsthand would be just as well. Go for a stroll in the woods or a park, have a picnic, or pick flowers for your altar. Be present in the equinox and make a connection with the earth and its abundance.

Ostara Altar Decorations

+ Eggs
+ Rabbit figurines
+ Fresh flowers or new growth
+ Seeds
+ Spring colors
+ Pastel candles
+ Symbols of balance
+ Representations of bees, ladybugs, and caterpillars

---

21. Connor, *Ostara*, 28, 33.

Beltane

Northern Hemisphere: May 1

Southern Hemisphere: November 1

Beltane, pronounced BEL-tayn, occurs on May 1 in the Northern Hemisphere and is one of the four greater sabbats. This sabbat, which sits opposite of Samhain on the Wheel of the Year, marks the beginning of the light half of the year. Beltane is thought to have been influenced by several ancient festivals that include Celtic, Roman, Greek, and Norse cultures.[22] Many of these festivals had an emphasis on blessings for the upcoming season as well as on fertility, and the Beltane festival that we know today has a similar focus. Beltane's focus is on the coming together of the god and the goddess, and it is a combination of their respective masculine and feminine energies. This celebration is one of union, abundance, fertility, and vitality.[23]

Beltane, like Samhain, is a fire festival. *Beltane* itself is a Celtic word meaning "bright fire," and as such, this sabbat is deeply rooted in this element.[24] The Celts would light the balefire on the eve of Beltane, although tradition varies depending on location. The fire was symbolic of the sun and the return of summer. Aside from lighting the balefire, Beltane was celebrated with a feast, dancing, and, due to the emphasis on fertility, carnal movement and activities. Many of the festivals that inspired Beltane were known for both their frolicking and their fornicating, and as such, Beltane is a free-spirited celebration that has many sexual aspects and representations.

Another common element of Beltane is the typically wooden Maypole that has ribbons flowing from the top. The Maypole is considered phallic in nature by many and a nod to the fertility element within the sabbat.[25] Dancing occurs around the Maypole until the ribbons are intertwined, representing the marriage between the god and goddess. As such, another common influence of this time is the Green Man, who is connected to Cernunnos, or the Horned God.[26] In Wicca, this deity is the representation of masculine energy as well as fertility.

---

22. Wigington, "Beltane History."
23. Cunningham, *Wicca*, 69.
24. "A Detailed History of Beltane."
25. History.com editors, "May Day."
26. Mark, "Wheel of The Year."

There are other ways to celebrate this sabbat, and one of those ways is to decorate a May bush. A May bush is erected either on the eve of Beltane or the day of and is then decorated with ribbons, painted eggshells, and flowers. Like during other sabbats, a feast is commonly held to celebrate, and Beltane bannock is a traditional bread for this sabbat. It is made with oatmeal and has a flat appearance. It was thought that eating bannock would ensure abundance for your crops and livestock.

Beltane Altar Decorations

- Chalice
- Antlers or horns
- Flowers
- Nuts, berries, and fruits
- Fire
- Sword or athame
- Ribbons
- Spring-colored candles, such as greens and yellow
- Bannock

Litha

Northern Hemisphere: June 21 to 22
Southern Hemisphere: December 21 to 22

Litha, pronounced LI-thuh, occurs on the Summer Solstice each year, which falls somewhere around June 21 in the Northern Hemisphere, depending on the year. It is also known as Midsummer. Because Litha takes place on the Summer Solstice, meaning the days will grow shorter until Yule, the sabbat is seen as another battle between light and dark. As with Yule, this is personified in the fight between the Oak King (light) and the Holly King (dark). On this solstice, the Holly King wins.[27]

The origins of Litha aren't exactly clear, but there is historical documentation that many civilizations celebrated the Summer Solstice. Prior to Christianity, Pagan groups, such as Germanic and Celtic groups, would celebrate the solstice with bonfires. These bonfires were an offering to the sun and used to encourage the successful

---

27. Blake, *Midsummer*, 7.

growth of crops, but they also served the purpose of keeping evil or malicious forces at bay.[28] The name *Litha* itself appears to have first been recorded in 725 by Bede, a monk and scholar, in his work the *De temporum ratione*, which translates to "On the Reckoning of Time." In this work, he used the term *Litha* to describe the period around June and July. However, the term was not associated with the sabbat we know today until the 1970s through the works of Aidan Kelly.[29]

Litha is a time when the goddess, impregnated at Beltane, is seen as Mother Earth and is ripe with fertility. The world is in full bloom. Simultaneously, the god is at the height of his power, be it in the form of the sun god or Green Man. While Litha is a solar-oriented sabbat, it also represents the balance of fire and water. This is an acknowledgment of the fact that water promotes growth. After all, the watering of crops produces new life. Flowers are also deeply symbolic of this sabbat as they represent the nature of the sabbat: growth, life, and abundance. Herbs are at the height of their power at this time, and this is a good time to collect them for later use. In fact, magick itself is thought to be more potent during this time.

With this being the Summer Solstice, it goes without saying that one of the best ways to celebrate Litha is to get outdoors. When possible, bask in the sunlight, visit the beach or a body of water, and connect with the elements of nature. June is also historically a popular time for weddings or their Pagan counterpart, which is called a handfasting. If you were planning a union, this time of year may be an optimal time for it to take place.

For Litha, rituals can be performed at high noon or at sunrise to connect with the solar energy of this sabbat. With the sun being a fundamental component of this sabbat, you can also work with solar deities if they have a place in your practice. Even if you don't work with deities, this can still be a time for worshipping the sun. This solar focus means it would also be a perfect time to charge your crystals in the sun, but be mindful of those that will fade, such as amethyst and citrine. The sun is at its most potent at this time. The solar emphasis and the corresponding element of fire means a bonfire can also be a great way to celebrate.

---

28. History.com Editors, "Summer Solstice."
29. Kelly, "About Naming Ostara, Litha, and Mabon."

Litha Altar Decorations

+ God's-eyes
+ Sun representations
+ Symbols of light and dark
+ Brightly colored candles
+ Brightly colored altar cloths
+ Flowers

Lammas

Northern Hemisphere: August 1

Southern Hemisphere: February 1

Lammas, pronounced LAH-mus, often called Lughnasadh, pronounced LOO-nah-sah, is celebrated on August 1 in the Northern Hemisphere. This sabbat is a celebration between the midpoint of the Summer Solstice and the Autumn Equinox. As I'm sure you may have guessed, this means the celebration is one of the greater sabbats.

While Lammas was originally an Anglo-Saxon tradition that celebrated the first harvest, Lughnasadh comes from Irish traditions that honored the harvest along with the Celtic god Lugh.[30] Lugh, who was a master craftsman, had ties with harvest and grains. This association is said to be tied back to the funeral of his foster mother, which is where he held a harvest fair in her honor.[31] The word *Lammas* itself means "loaf mass," which speaks to the harvesting of grains for bread. Throughout history, the growth cycle of grain was considered symbolic of life and death. While these two festivals had their differences, the focus on harvest was consistent, and today's Lammas is an amalgamation of the two.

Lammas is the last of the fire festivals, but it is also the first harvest festival as it is honored by cutting the first grain of the year, and it is a time to celebrate a successful harvest. This can also be the time of year to reap the benefits of prior hard work, and it does not need to relate directly to the harvesting of crops, especially since many of us are not as agriculturally focused as our ancestors. But

---

30. Mankey, *Witch's Wheel of the Year*, 251.
31. Cartwright, "Lugh."

keeping in tune with the celebration's roots, a feast to honor the literal or figurative harvest is in order. After all, what Pagan celebration is complete without a feast? Some good foods to include in your celebration are harvested foods, meads, and wines. Lammas bread can be represented by wheat and grains.

The historical celebration of Lugh, the master craftsman and artisan, also makes this sabbat a particularly good time to get crafty, and it's even better if you can incorporate the other elements of Lammas as you do so. You could make a decorative display of grains in a vase to place somewhere around your home or on your altar, or alternatively you can create a wreath for your home from dried corn or grain. Do not limit yourself, though. If you have a talent, today is a day to spend honoring that talent and creating.

Lammas Altar Decorations
+ Corn
+ Wheat or other grains
+ Baskets of harvested foods
+ Wine, vines, or grapes
+ Artisan crafts
+ Candles in oranges, browns, and reds
+ Cornflowers or sunflowers
+ Fire

MABON
Northern Hemisphere: September 20 to 23
Southern Hemisphere: March 20 to 22

Mabon, pronounced MAY-bonn, is also known as the Autumn Equinox or Midharvest Festival. Since it takes place on the equinox, it does not fall on a set day, and it's typically sometime between September 20 to 23 in the Northern Hemisphere. As an equinox, this is also a day when light and dark are equal, and because of this, there is a sense of balance.

Mabon is the second harvest festival. The name of this sabbat is another that originates from the work of Aidan Kelly.[32] While the name *Mabon* does not

---

32. Kelly, "About Naming Ostara, Litha, and Mabon."

coincide with the names of any historical festivals, there is evidence that harvest festivals took place near the Autumn Equinox in several cultures. One such celebration was called harvest home, and it took place in much of Europe. This celebration, sometimes referred to as Ingathering, was a time of joy surrounding the harvest. While harvesters prepared for the winter, they would make games out of the work, and the festivities extended throughout the town. Doors were decked with wreathes, games were played, and a feast was had.[33]

As such, Mabon is a time for gratitude and being thankful for the plentiful bounty of Mother Earth. With this in mind, you can host a harvest dinner—much like a Thanksgiving feast. In fact, Mabon is often thought of as the "Thanksgiving of Pagans." Focus on foods that are in season and freshly harvested in your location. Being the Pagan Thanksgiving, this is a time to give thanks and express gratitude. Even if throwing an exorbitant feast is not on the docket, you could simply end your meal by sharing why you're grateful.

This is another sabbat that can be honored by spending time outdoors, particularly since the cooler days will soon be here. Go for a walk and connect with the beauty and riches that are only found outside the confines of your four walls. You can use this stroll to collect fallen leaves and acorns for your altar. You do not have to stop at your altar, though. Get in the spirit of the season by decorating your home for autumn.

Mabon Altar Decorations

+ Apples
+ Cornucopias
+ Candles in reds, oranges, browns, golds, and coppers
+ Fallen leaves
+ Seeds
+ Pine cones
+ Pumpkins and other gourds
+ Crystals such as citrine, amber, and cat's-eye
+ Flowers such as sunflowers and marigolds

---

33. Rajchel, *Mabon*, 28.

makinᏳ it your own

While I've touched briefly on the historical and modern celebrations of these sabbats, I encourage you to make them your own. Each sabbat will look different for every individual, and personalizing your celebration will assist you in building a practice that you find personally fulfilling. To make these sabbats your own, tune in to the seasons of your local landscape during these time periods. Allow this relationship with the spirit of your area to guide you in creating your own connection with these festivals. You can also tune in to the overall themes of the season. For instance, winter is considered a time of death, whereas spring has an emphasis on rebirth. Keep this in mind and use these times to check in with yourself and determine what changes could be made in your life. Identify what you need to release or what areas in which you feel you could grow. Remember, these are merely guidelines and extractions from each of these celebrations. If you do not resonate with a sabbat, skip it. You make the rules. Here is a quick review of the sabbats with major themes for you to build on and explore:

Samhain: The theme of this sabbat is death and remembrance. While this is a time to honor your ancestors and loved ones, it's also a time to reflect on the year behind you and celebrate all that has been achieved. This would be an excellent time to practice tarot, or other divination, for an overview of the year ahead and a recap of the year past. You should use this reading to assess what to leave behind you as well as what's to come.

Yule: This is the time to clear the slate from the previous rotations and begin again. Death and rebirth have a place in Yule as well as other sabbats. Take the time to consider what you are ready to leave behind. This is a good time to practice banishing magick and cord-cutting rituals.

Imbolc: The theme of Imbolc is renewal and purification, particularly of the home and hearth. This is a time of tidying up our space and our mind; it is a time to shake off winter and emerge anew. This would be a good time to cleanse your home with whichever method you prefer. Make banishing sprays, utilize floor washes, or smoke cleanse your home with herb bundles or incense.

Ostara: Ostara builds on the themes of Imbolc, but the overarching theme of Ostara is rebirth. Once you have cleared your slate and cleansed your living space—as well as yourself—it is time to work toward personal growth as nature does the same. Take time to sit with yourself. Where are you at, and where would you like to be? It is time to plant those seeds and start your own process of growth. This would be an excellent time to perform manifestation magick in unison with pursuing your goals.

Beltane: The themes of Beltane are joy and fertility. Spring has sprung, and summer is around the corner. As such, the spirit of Beltane is jubilant and lighthearted. Be kind to yourself and have fun. Take a trip and shake things up, or do something otherwise spontaneous! Take a moment to feel alive. This is a potent time for magick, so if you have spellwork you have been waiting to perform, this is a great time to tap into the energy around you.

Litha: Litha occurs on the Summer Solstice, making it the longest day of the year. Earth is at its peak moment, so take the time to recognize your own abundance, your own peak moments of the year, and express gratitude. This would be an excellent time to perform magick that concerns abundance in whatever presents itself to you and what you value.

Lammas: Lammas was a period of uncertainty in ancient civilizations. Would their livelihood survive the impending winter? Sit with your own fears about things to come. Analyze the areas in your life that are holding you back, focus on how they may force you to live from a place of uncertainty, and address those fears to the best of your ability. This is also a good time for you to focus on shadow work, which we will cover in chapter 14, as well as protection magick.

Mabon: Mabon is a time of balance and reflection. Think about the areas in your life that feel off-center. How can these be recalibrated for the better? Mabon is also a time of gratitude. Consider using this time to start a gratitude journal where you list something you are grateful for each day. For most of the Northern Hemisphere, this is a time when warm weather is ending, soon to be replaced by cooler days. As such, this makes it a perfect time for evaluating our lives and what we would like to change and leave behind with the season.

Broom Closet Witch Tips

Several sabbats, including Yule, Ostara, and Samhain, have holidays that take place at similar points in the seasons.

When it comes to Yule, many of the typical Christmas traditions have roots in Pagan traditions, so celebrating Yule can often fly under the radar unless explicitly stated. Caroling? Kissing under the mistletoe? Decking the halls and hanging ornaments? All Pagan in origin. If you are operating in the broom closet, decorate your Yule tree or log with glee under the guise of celebrating Christmas.

The same can be said for Ostara. You have likely noticed that many of the Ostara and Easter celebrations go hand in hand. After all, Ostara occurs around the time of Easter and makes use of eggs and rabbits. You can decorate and craft for this sabbat while blending in seamlessly with the festivities of Easter.

Samhain takes place on the same day as Halloween, and many of the decorations used on Halloween can be used for honoring Samhain as well. Who is to say if the strategically placed Halloween decor is really an altar? Plausible deniability.

The act of going outdoors during the solstices and equinoxes, weather permitting, is a great way to honor the sabbats that don't occur next to "major" holidays. Skim the associations for each sabbat you'd like to recognize to determine small, subtle ways to incorporate and honor them in your practice. Every sabbat doesn't need to be met with a large production, and you may find you don't connect with some or any of them. That is absolutely fine, and it doesn't make you any less of a witch.

tools of
the trade

the first occult shop I ever entered was on a trip to New Orleans. This was during my childhood, and it became the first of many as New Orleans is a city with magick that is felt and understood by many at a cellular level. The shop itself was off a cobblestone street, tucked neatly away between larger tourist shops, bars, and restaurants. The store was a narrow shop, but the shelves were filled from bottom to top with items I wouldn't have been able to identify at the time. Nevertheless, they were intriguing. In fact, they were so intriguing I had to know more.

If you have ever entered a quaint occult shop yourself and wondered what the items displayed were for, this chapter is for you. While I will review the items in general, giving basic descriptions, I will also focus on ways you can use these tools in your practice. Based on this information, you can then decide which tools you would like to welcome into your path, assuming you choose to utilize tools at all. Tools are not necessary, particularly at the beginning of your journey, but they can be helpful.

The descriptions you will find here are, admittedly, largely Wiccan-influenced in terms of the associations and names used. However, there is some crossover between Wiccan traditions and more eclectic or traditional styles of witchcraft. I will provide their associations to the elements and cardinal directions as well as their associations to masculine and feminine energy.

Oftentimes, objects are associated with masculine or feminine energy, and it's largely due to symbolism. The masculine objects will frequently be phallic in nature, while feminine objects will typically have a space that is thought to represent the womb. It's worth noting that all humans have both of these energies within themselves to varying degrees, and these terms do not mean "man" or "woman." Masculine energy is considered to be one of drive, logic, and external, whereas feminine energy is more collaborative, intuitive, and internal. If the idea of these concepts seems dated to you, they are certainly not required for practice.

What is most important about these items is your personal connection to them. While the tools will retain a portion of your energy through repeated use, they do not come with their own power. Remember: the tools are not the magick; the magick is you.

atHame

An athame, pronounced AH-thuh-may or ah-THAH-may, depending on whom you ask, is a ritual tool that is used to direct energy. This can also be referred to as a ritual knife. An athame is considered masculine in nature and, depending on tradition, it represents either the element of air or the element of fire. While it is stated in some traditions that an athame should be dulled and double-edged with a dark handle, this is not necessary. If you find yourself drawn to a particular knife, that's okay; do not limit yourself to the traditional description. Personally, my most prized athame is a hand-carved athame made entirely of wood—blade and all.

Ways to Use

- ✦ The most popular and traditional use of an athame is to direct energy. This is often done in circle casting, and an athame can also be used to exit a circle.
- ✦ When directing energy, an athame can be used in two directions. It can draw the energy inward, or toward you, and direct energy outward, or away from you.
- ✦ An athame can also be used to cut energetic cords. This is done symbolically by envisioning the energetic ties to a person or thing and severing the ties with the blade.

◆ While some traditions state that an athame is not to be used for physical cutting, newer traditions make some exceptions for this and use the athame to cut sacred herbs or in kitchen witchery. If you choose to use your athame to physically cut materials, keep in mind that it will need to be cleansed on both a practical and metaphysical level.

BELL

Bells are often overlooked tools, but that doesn't negate their usefulness. This tool can come in many shapes and sizes, and it is generally made from metal with the most frequent composition being a combination of copper and tin. While many of the bells commonly used are a type of hand bell, which consists of a hallowed cup containing a clapper with a handle atop, there are several other types of bells, including circular bells, also called sleigh bells, and wind chimes.

The type of bell you use is not important because it's the sound the bell produces that creates change. In short, bells are used in rituals to change the vibrations and frequencies of the rooms. Bells can also be hung around entryways, and many witches hang bells on their doors as an act of protection for their homes. These bells are often referred to as "witches' bells," and they are created by attaching several smaller bells to a circular hoop.

Ways to Use

◆ Ringing a bell can be a cleansing action as it moves stagnant energy while simultaneously evoking positive energy. Bells can also be rung before spellwork or rituals.

◆ The act of ringing a bell produces an immediate change. Silence is broken, and the world around you is filled with a vibration of chiming. This powerful symbolism can be utilized in your workings.

◆ Bells can also be used to invoke spirits. Bells have a long-standing place in history and, as such, are powerful tools for drawing forth certain spirits.

◆ In the same right, bells can also be used to drive away spirits who do not align with the bell's frequency, and they can be used as a form of protection against unwanted spirits.

BOLINE

A boline is a working knife, and it is the laborer tool counterpart to the athame. While athames are used in rituals, bolines serve a more practical use. That said, my own boline is kept separately from my other knives and stored with the rest of my tools.

Traditionally, bolines were to have white handles and crescent blades, but much like with the athame's composition, this is not necessary. My own stand-in boline is a foldable pocketknife. If you wish to incorporate a boline into your practice, find a blade that speaks to you that can be easily used for various purposes.

Ways to Use

- As you have read under the athame section, the jury is still out on whether or not you should use an athame for the act of physical cutting in magickal work. If you do not wish to use an athame, a boline is a wonderful tool to add to your collection.
- A boline can be used to inscribe candles with intentions, such as words or sigils, when you are practicing candle magick and carve any other material that you may work with.
- A boline is a wonderful tool to gather and cut sacred herbs with.
- Use this tool to cut ribbons and cords in the necessary spells and rituals, such as cord-cutting and binding spells.

BROOM

Brooms are the one item seemingly most associated with witches given that witches are frequently depicted riding them in both art and literature from yesteryear to today. Although that is not its primary use in present day, the broom is still a handy tool in a witch's arsenal. After all, this is not an ordinary broom used for sweeping kitchen floors. Associated with water, this magickal broom will be sacred to your practice.

You may hear the terms *broom* and *besom* used interchangeably. *Besom* is a word that is English in origin, and it was what this tool was originally called. The term *broom*, which corresponds with the plant material used in the tool's creation, eventually replaced the term *besom* in popularity. You can use whichever term you feel most drawn to.

Ways to Use

+ The primary function of a broom or besom is purification, which is why it is linked to the element of water. Tidy your work space before you perform any spellwork or rituals by sweeping away and clearing energy with your besom.

+ While you do not want to literally sweep the floors with a broom, you can perform a cleansing ritual by sweeping above the floors without letting the bristles touch the ground. Remember, this is a sacred tool, and it is not to be confused with your average broom.

+ Besoms are also used as protection. In folklore, a broom laid across a doorway would prevent negativity from entering your home. You can practice this by hanging a broom over an entryway or leaving a broom behind a door.

CAULDRON

Visions of witches riding off under the moonlight on their broomsticks are popularly depicted in lore, and so are images of witches huddled around cauldrons crafting potions. While I've yet to determine how to convert my method of transportation to broom powered, I've certainly used my cauldrons for a potion or two.

The cauldron is a vessel made of iron that is used to create magick. It is symbolic of the goddess, fertility, and the element of water. The cauldron is a staple for witches, and it is used for many purposes depending on a person's practice. It can be used for liquids and fire, which makes it a versatile tool in one's workings.

Ways to Use

+ A cauldron can be used in spellwork that requires boiling liquids. In my own practice, I often use a cauldron to make particular waters to use in later spellwork, such as rose water or prosperity water.

+ It is also a useful tool to use in burning loose incense. If you wish to protect your cauldron, you can line the bottom with a layer of salt and place the lit charcoal disc on it.

+ Don't limit your cauldron to incense. It's also a fantastic tool to have for spells that require you to burn other items. For example, someday you might want to burn bay leaves as messages for manifestations and banishing.

CUP

A cup, or chalice, is another tool that may be useful for your practice, particularly on your altar. A chalice is defined as a large cup or goblet, and the term you use will depend upon personal preference and tradition. The cup symbolizes the goddess and fertility and is associated with the element of water. The material used for the cup is not as important as its symbolism.

Scott Cunningham, Wiccan practitioner and author whose books on the craft were among the first I read, refers to a cup as a cauldron with a stem in his book *Wicca: Guide for The Solitary Practitioner*.[34] I must agree with this assessment as many of the correspondences for the cup and cauldron are perilously close.

Ways to Use

+ If your chalice is made of metal, you can use it to burn loose incense blends. As with the cauldron, you can line the bottom with salt to protect it.

+ A chalice can be used as a container to create potions in, combining both dry and wet ingredients.

+ When it comes to working with the elements, a chalice is an excellent representation to include on your altar for the element of water.

+ It can be used in rituals or spellwork that requires liquids, such as water or wine, to be consumed, either literally or figuratively, or left on your altar as offerings for ancestors, spirits, or deities.

---

34. Cunningham, *Wicca*, 35.

pentacle

The pentacle, which is often confused for the pentagram, is the five-pointed star enclosed within a circle. These points represent earth, air, fire, water, and spirit. The pentacle is an often-misunderstood symbol to those who aren't familiar with it. The pentacle is not a symbol of malice. Rather, it is a symbol that is often used for protection.

A pentacle can be included on your altar in several forms, such as an altar tile or charm. It can even be engraved in one of your working items. The pentacle can also often be included in an altar space for its devotional significance. The symbol itself is sacred to many practitioners and holds within its design a sacred power. Due to the simplicity of its design, it's an easy symbol to draw; the pencil doesn't even need to lift from the paper. You can tap into your creativity and create your own. One of my favorite pentacles is one I crafted out of floral wire and crystal beads.

Ways to Use

- The pentacle is used for evocation, but in some traditions, this can be referred to as an "invoking pentagram," which is performed by drawing out the pentagram and calling forth the elements, energies, or spirits you wish to use during your working.
- Utilize the pentacle as a symbol of protection by wearing it on your person or hanging it in your space.
- A pentacle can be drawn or painted on items, such as journals, or inscribed on items, such as candles, to imbue them with protection and connection to the elements.

WAND

A wand is a tool that is associated with the element of air or fire, depending on your tradition. A wand is considered masculine in nature, and this is due to its distinctly phallic shape.

Certain traditions specify both a length and material, namely wood, to be used for the wand, but this isn't something I adhere to, and it's the same for many modern practitioners. Wands can be made from several different types of material, such as crystal, metal, or glass, and they do not necessarily have to be plain. Depending on the material, wands can be engraved or adorned with crystals and other items. If you'd like to add a little more pizzazz to your own wand, feel free to get creative. Just know that you should pick your wand materials based on what you connect with the most.

Ways to Use

- A wand's primary use is to direct energy, much like the athame, and wands are often used to cast a circle or charge an item.
- As a tool that directs energy, a wand is wonderful to use in an "invoking pentagram" ritual, meaning the pentagram would not be drawn physically but in midair with the wand.
- Wands are also useful for activating your sigils or intentions. Simply use the wand's tip to create the shape of the symbol or the words in the air.

Broom Closet Witch Tips

Make this no secret: tools are not necessary to be an efficient witch. Tools that are used to direct energy, such as athames and wands, can simply be replaced with your hands. After all, you can just as easily use your fingers and palms to point and channel energy. While these tools can assist you in your workings, they are not requirements. However, it shouldn't be too difficult to play off a wand as book or movie memorabilia.

Certain items, such as bells, brooms, cups, and even bolines, are rather unassuming on their own. Bells are commonplace items, brooms are used to sweep floors, cups are necessary for drinking, and a pocket-knife is a practical tool to have on hand. If you find yourself called to any of these items, you can easily blend them into the background so they do not scream, "They are a witch!" to any potential bystanders. If you do keep tools, they can be placed in a box and discretely stored underneath your bed or in your closet.

tнe eLeмeɴтs

Step outdoors for a moment to connect. Feel the energy around you. Feel the earth below you and the sky above, the fire within you and the air around you. While you are a fundamental source of energy for your practice, there is a plethora of magick that you can tap into outside of yourself and the confines your home.

In my own practice, I am reliant on a heavy dose of animism. What I mean by this is that I believe that a spirit and energy exist in objects, places, and things that may seem like inanimate objects to another person. Every tree has a story, and every home has a name. There is magick to be found in what others might consider mundane, and it is present if we look beneath the veil.

The key is to keep the concept of animism in mind when we approach our work with the four elements. While we can touch many of these elements on the physical plane, we can also access them on the energetic plane, and the following sections will go over ways to form an understanding and connection with the elements through both tangible and intangible means.

There is an intrinsic rhythm in the world around us that also exists within us. Before us, the elements work in unison to create the planet we inhabit, but they also reside inside us. Earth is beneath our feet but is also from where we emerged and where we will return. Air surrounds us but is also within our breath. Fire exists in roaring flames but exists, too, within our soul and our passions. Water fills the oceans, rivers, and seas but also quenches our thirst and soothes our spirit. We are one, and the elements are willing to assist us if we both ask and listen.

eartн

The earth is a generous source of energy. It is fertile, ripe with growth and abundance, and identifiable. Earth is the planet we inhabit, after all, and earth surrounds us. It is the ground beneath our feet, the trees and mountains on the horizon, the plants in our gardens, and the sands on our shores. The earth, though appearing still, is in constant motion. It is in a continuous state of life, renewal, and rebirth. When we think of the earth, we think of its heavy and tangible nature. We think of grounding and the consistent regeneration of life.

North is the direction of this element, and the signs associated with this element are Taurus, Virgo, and Capricorn. These signs are known for their down-to-earth nature, pragmatism, and stability, much like the earth itself. Earth is also connected to the suit of pentacles in tarot, as this suit concerns the material world, finance, and practicality. Even outside of the tarot, earth is represented by pentacles.

When we wish to connect to the element of earth, all we have to do is step outdoors. Whether we live in rural areas, suburbs, or cities, the earth is beneath our feet. If the option is available, we can plant our feet directly on the grass or soil for a recharge. We can climb a mountain, visit a park, or hike a trail. We can plant our own garden or pluck flowers. We can consume the healthy foods the earth provides. Working with the element of earth can be simple. It does not have to be elaborate or ceremonial. There is magick to be found in simplicity and connection with the world around us.

Earth Magick with Metals

Metals are sometimes overlooked in magick, but they are a powerful part of the earth. Metals are extracted from ore, which is a naturally occurring material in the earth's crust. In practice, people often make pendulums out of specific metals, which I will discuss in detail in chapter 11, with each pendulum embodying the correspondence of its particular metal. Being intentional about what our jewelry is made out of is another easy and popular way to use the magick of metal. Different types of metal also make suitable materials to use for talismans, and metal can also be used in spell jars and sachets. While the metal itself can correspond with other elements, it is still material of the earth. Use these following metals as you see fit in your own practice, keeping in mind that some are highly toxic and must be handled with extreme care.

Copper: Copper corresponds with Venus and has properties of love and pleasure.

Gold: Gold corresponds with the sun and has properties of prosperity and success.

Iron: Iron corresponds with Mars and has properties of victory and success.

Lead: Lead corresponds with Saturn and has properties of healing and protection.

    Note: Lead is highly toxic.

Silver: Silver corresponds with the moon and has psychic and intuitive properties.

Tin: Tin corresponds with Jupiter and has properties of guidance and abundance.

Earth Magick with Trees

When it comes to the earth's other offerings, trees are often overlooked too. Most people gravitate toward crystals or herbs instead, but trees really are a wonderful addition to your practice. Plus, their leaves and other offerings are often easy to source.

Each tree has its own correspondences that can complement your spellwork. Wands, athames, staffs, altar tiles, and other tools can be crafted using specific types of wood to bring their correspondences into your practice. Further, you could choose a particular type of wood for your altar or the furniture you place around your home. On a smaller scale, the leaves and fruits of trees can also be used in spellwork, and that's just scratching the surface. Scott Cunningham's *Encyclopedia of Magical Herbs* has been a staple in my practice for years. As such, I've compiled this list from the text to assist you in exploring the use of these trees in your own practice.

Ash: Ash trees are known to be protective trees that are good for balance, communication, creativity, growth, healing, and intuition.

Bamboo: Bamboo trees are protective trees with properties of strength, luck, peace, wisdom, and harmony.

Birch: Birch trees can be used for protection, abundance, focus, purification, healing, inspiration, intuition, and new beginnings.

Cedar: Cedar trees are good for prosperity as well as longevity, success, love, fidelity, purification, release, wisdom, and strength.

Cypress: Cypress trees are good for protection as well as strength, transformation, heightening awareness, and processing grief.

Elm: Elm trees are good for protection as well as attraction, changes, justice, loyalty, psychic abilities, and wisdom.

Eucalyptus: Eucalyptus trees are known for their healing properties as well as being good for banishing, communication, psychic abilities, purification, protection, and strength.

Juniper: Juniper trees are good for protection as well as abundance, harmony, success, transformation, and prosperity.

Maple: Maple trees are good for love as well as divination, abundance, dream work, grief, love, release, and wisdom.

Mulberry: Mulberry trees are good for wisdom as well as knowledge, creativity, luck, protection, and success.

Oak: Oak trees are trees of strength, healing, endurance, fidelity, manifestation, protection, spirit guides, and prosperity.

Palm: Palm trees are good for strength as well as wisdom, abundance, courage, healing, hope, purification, success, and protection.

Pine: Pine trees are good for prosperity as well as good fortune, abundance, banishing, binding, communication, manifestation, psychic abilities, strength, and health.

Rowan: Rowan trees are good for protection as well as strength, astral travel, binding, divination, defense, inspiration, knowledge, and success.

Willow: Willow trees are good for wishes as well as protection, adaptability, divination, intuition, prophecy, strength, and healing.[35]

---

35. Cunningham, *Cunningham's Encyclopedia of Magical Herbs*.

Earth Altar

There may be a time when you would like to build an altar specifically to honor the element of earth. This could be due to your connection with the element or a specific ritual, or perhaps you work with a particular deity that corresponds with the element. Whatever the case may be, you can begin the process by sourcing materials that correspond with the element. Arrange them on your altar in a way you find aesthetically pleasing that also helps the energy flow best. Allow your intuition to guide you. You can also make sure your tools are made from certain metals or wood, or you can use those representations of the element as offerings. Pentacles can symbolize the element, too, and if you are crafty, you can create them out of earth elements, such as twigs, plants, crystals, or flowers.

What to Include on an Earth Altar
+ Crystals
+ Dirt
+ Earthy foods
+ Herbs
+ Metal
+ Pentacles
+ Plants and flowers
+ Representations of earth deities, such as Gaia or Danu
+ Salt
+ Wood

air

Air is an element that is not often seen, but it surrounds us at all times. We can feel its presence on a windy day, and we consume it rhythmically to sustain life. Thanks to this, focusing on our breath (and breath work as a whole) is one of the easiest ways to connect with the element of air. Feel the air. Feel it fill your lungs. Concentrate on your breath as it reaches deep within you. Air envelops you.

When wanting to connect with the element of air and also your own power, you can go outside and channel your energy into directing the wind. This no-frills practice only involves channeling your energy into guiding the wind. You don't need any supplies aside from yourself and the outdoors. Simply focus on the direction you want the wind to blow. This practice is a good starting point for honing your abilities and growing confidence with them. Through this simple practice, you can tap into the element of air at a moment's notice.

Smoke is also associated with this element, so if you need to channel air, you can light incense or burn herb bundles to call the element forth. However, when it comes to elemental magick, the ideal place to connect with an element is outside. Immerse yourself in nature to connect with this element in its full glory.

The east is the direction associated with this element, and the signs that are associated with the element are Gemini, Libra, and Aquarius. These signs are known for their sociability, intellect, and lightheartedness. The element of air in the tarot is represented by the suit of swords, and this suit represents matters of the mind, ideas, and challenges. Outside of the tarot, the element of air can be represented by athames and swords, though some traditions attribute air to wands. This, of course, depends on how you view the tools themselves. If you are an avid tarot reader, you are likely to settle on swords (and athames) corresponding with air. Some view the sharpness of the blade as an association with intellect and, therefore, the element of air. On the other hand, the lightness of wands, the fact they're wielded through the air, and their association with branches lends to others viewing them as being associated with air. There is no definitive answer, so you can choose what makes the most sense for you.

Air Magick

The direction that the wind blows brings a particular type of energy. If you are interested in working with the wind, you can determine which way the wind blows by simply stepping outside. However, if you do not want to go outside with your compass and run tests, weather apps and websites can provide this information for you.

When using these directions, you can be as elaborate or as simple as you would like. If you have a specific intention, you can combine candle magick with wind magick by dressing your candle and taking it outdoors for the wind to extinguish its flame and send the intention outward toward manifestation. The wind you would want to use depends on the type of spellwork you are doing. Read through the following list to determine what wind would serve your purpose the best.

North: Winds from the north correspond with death, releasing, and breaking habits.

East: Winds from the east correspond with renewal, intellect, and strength.

South: Winds from the south correspond with potency, fire energy, and action.

West: Winds from the west correspond with healing, fertility, and purification.

Air Altar

If air is dominant in your chart, you are honoring deities associated with the element of air, or you already have an altar for each other element, you may want to create an altar that is specific to air. If possible, you should place this altar in the element's corresponding direction of the east, and you should adorn this altar with items that are representative of the element. You could also add tools with the association of air, such as bells, incense, wands, or athames (depending on the tradition), as well as candles in colors that correspond with this element, such as yellow, white, purple, and blue. Arrange your altar intuitively with the understanding that there is no proper way to set up *your* altar. Tune in with the energy between the items, and let your intuition guide you.

What to Include on an Air Altar

- Athames or wands (or both)
- Bells
- Besoms
- Feathers
- Incense
- Representations of air deities, such as Aeolus or Aether
- Representations of fae
- Symbols of birds and other winged animals
- Yellow, white, purple, and blue candles

fire

In nature, lightning striking the ground can create wildfires, but often we create it. We have invited fire into our homes to cook our food and heat our rooms for hundreds of years. Fire is a clever combination of oxygen, heat, and fuel, but connecting with the element of fire can be as simple as lighting a candle. If the option is available, a fire indoors or outdoors is an excellent way to draw this element forward. The fire itself is mesmerizing and meditative.

The direction associated with the element of fire is the south, and the signs that correspond with this element are Aries, Leo, and Sagittarius. These signs are known for their driven, fiery nature as well as their endurance and strength. Within the tarot, the element of fire is represented by the suit of wands, and this suit involves action and motivation. Much like what was covered in the air section, whether or not a wand or athame represents the element of fire is much debated.

In my own practice, I use athames as a representation of fire. This is likely due to the fact that tarot wasn't a part of my practice for many years, so I didn't have the association provided by the deck to guide my connection. I've also always been deeply intrigued by forging; the association between the blade and fire was a natural connection to me. That said, go with whatever feels right to you.

Fire Magick

Fire itself has many associations and, because of this, can have many uses within your practice. Fire can be destructive and can assist in destroying bonds that you no longer wish to sustain. In the same vein, fire can also be considered transformative, and it can be used when you need to bring about changes in your life to reach the next level. Fire is heavily associated with passion and creativity, so you can channel this energy into spellwork to help amplify these traits within yourself or others. Fire is also a sign of strength and energy, and it can be used in spellwork to bring these energies to the forefront too. Consider what you feel when you envision fire; it has many correspondences that you can use in your spellwork.

Fire Altar

As with earth and air, your reasons for creating a fire altar can vary, but if you need to connect further with the element of fire within your own practice, this is a great way to do so. When creating this altar, you can represent fire in both its literal and figurative forms. Candles make a great addition to a fire altar, and so do matches, lighters, and incense. The fire element also corresponds with the sun, so you can represent this solar energy by using figures of the sun itself or stones that are red or orange. My particular favorite for this is sunstone, but you have many more stones to choose from. Figurines of dragons as well as deities with fire associations would pair well with this altar. An altar cloth in red or orange would be a great choice to place your items on, too, and you can represent fire by using an athame, a wand, or both—it all depends on your personal association.

What to Include on a Fire Altar

+ Athames or wands (or both)
+ Candles
+ Incense
+ Matches and lighters
+ Red or orange cloth
+ Representations of dragons
+ Representations of fire deities, such as Hestia or Brigid
+ Sun imagery
+ Sunstone and other red or orange stones

WATER

Water is another vital element that we need to exist. Water is an expansive element, and its various depths, its changing tides, and its overall mysterious nature lend a hand to its associations. Water is deeply associated with psychic abilities and enhanced intuition, though it is not necessary to have water placements within your natal chart to have or to harness these abilities. As water is fluid, there is an association of movement attributed to the element. Water itself is adaptive, as it can exist in many forms, and it is a wonderful purifier and healer as well.

The direction associated with the element of water is west, and the signs for this element are Cancer, Scorpio, and Pisces. These signs are known for their depth, intuition, and creativity. In tarot, the suit of cups represents water, and those cards typically revolve around emotions, relationships, and matters of the heart. Outside of the tarot, the element of water is associated with cups, chalices, and cauldrons. Basically any vessel in which water can be collected can be associated with the element.

Water Magick

While my personal chart, though fire dominant, is heavily saturated with water placements, it is my geographical location along the Emerald Coast that has made my spiritual use of water the most profound. I have never lived more than five miles from a shoreline, and when my soul is not at rest, you can find me there; I have turned to bodies of water in times of turmoil for as long as I can remember. For every personal loss, I find a vessel or a shore and connect with the element of water to restore my balance. Simply being close by allows me the ability to tap into the healing energy of this element.

If proximity to a natural body of water is a challenge, that is absolutely fine. Connecting with the element of water can be as simple as drinking water. Along with moon water, I charge my normal drinking water with intentions as well. When charging water, the most important part of the process is visualization and focusing on what you are trying to achieve. To do this, place your hands close to your container of water and visualize channeling energy into the water. If you struggle coming up with visual images, audibly repeat your intention to yourself. If I want to add an additional boost to my water, I include a quartz crystal that corresponds to my intentions so it can lend its own properties.

For a more immersive approach connecting to this element, you can take a bath. This bath can be as simple, decadent, or spiritual as you choose. If possible, swimming is a great way to connect with this element as well. What is most important about these methods is the act of visualization or otherwise feeling your personal connection to the energy. Your intention can be purification, healing, or embodying any number of this element's correspondences. If it is purification, envision anything that no longer serves you being rinsed away. If the intention is healing, focus on the water permeating your being until you have been restored. However, just being *in* water can be a highly restorative experience without any additional intentions. Assess your needs and plan accordingly.

Water Altar

Having a water altar can be an extremely useful way to connect with the element's intuitive and purifying energies. You can also create a water altar to honor deities that correspond with the element or to honor the element of water itself. To find inspiration for this altar, simply think of items with connections to oceans, lakes, and other bodies of water. Shells, driftwood, sand, seaweed, and other such items all make excellent additions to water altars. Chalices, cups, and cauldrons are also wonderful options. Water altars can be placed in the element's corresponding direction of west, but this is not absolutely necessary. Do what works best with the space you have available. If you work with a specific water deity or honor water nymphs, include figurines or representations of them. You can also add a blue altar cloth and place blue candles on top. My final suggestion is to even include several different types of water. Consider rainwater, ocean water, moon water, or even tap water. As with other elemental altars, arrange this one in a way that speaks to you. These suggestions do not make up an all-inclusive list; use any items that you are drawn to and associate with this element.

What to Include on a Water Altar

- Blue altar cloth
- Blue candles
- Cauldrons, chalices, and cups
- Driftwood
- Representations of water deities, such as Poseidon or Dione
- Representations of water nymphs
- Sand
- Shells
- Water

Broom Closet Witch Tips

Working with and honoring the elements can be a very simple and inconspicuous practice, and there are many discrete ways to represent the elements and create altars that will go undetected. The following list should give you inspiration for innocuous representations for each element.

Earth: Brown or green candles, crystals, dirt, plants, salt, and twigs

Air: Bells, bird figurines, blue or yellow candles, feathers, and incense

Fire: Candles, dragon and phoenix figurines, knives, and lighters and matches

Water: Blue candles, bowls, cups, pots, shells, and watering cans

Of course, probably the easiest and most inconspicuous way to honor the elements is to simply get outdoors. If possible, go for a walk on a sunny day somewhere near a body of water. In this method, the elements are literally represented all around you. The earth is located beneath your feet, the air is surrounding you, fire is in the sky in the form of the sun, and water is nearby. Honoring the elements doesn't have to be a difficult part of your practice. If you live in a city, find the nearest park that you can explore to remove yourself from the bustle and reconnect with nature.

Chapter Six

eLements
at work

While the last chapter introduced ways of identifying and connecting with the elements, this chapter will expand upon methods you can use to bring them to life in your practice. I will focus on the physical aspects of working with these elements, but more importantly, I will focus on what they mean and how to put your magick into action.

Much of witchcraft is symbolic, and the acts we perform have their own meanings. Often, a spell will call for an action that may leave the newcomer perplexed about the *why* behind it. More seasoned practitioners are often more than happy to assist, but the objective is for each person to be able to branch out and create their own brand of magick. However, to do this, they should ideally have a working knowledge of the symbolism of their actions—the *why*. This chapter is here to accomplish just that.

eartH maɡick IN actION

Bringing the element of earth into your practice on the physical plane is rather simple. It merely requires getting your hands dirty—quite literally. Find a space outdoors where you can put your hands in the soil. The action of touching and working with the dirt, coupled with your intention, is where the magick happens.

Burying

The earth is sacred. As such, dirt itself is a powerful tool. Dirt can be used for cleansing, protection, banishing, binding, and more. It is ripe with energy, and specific types of dirt have their own frequency. While I will go over different types of dirt to incorporate into your practice, this section will be specific to the *act* of burying in spellwork, which is often used to disperse and direct energy. When you bury a spell, you are continuing the energy as well as amplifying it with the element of earth. Burying an item is best when used for long-term spells.

When it comes to burying an object in witchcraft, another critical component to the *why* is location, location, location. If you wanted to enact protection for your home or attract good fortune, for example, you would bury an item nearby to keep the energy close and draw the spell to you. You could bury it in your yard or near your front door. The backyard would also suffice if you live in a suburb and don't feel like fielding your nosy neighbors' questions; if the backyard offers more privacy than your front yard, bury it there. If you live in a city or apartment building, burying the item in a houseplant would do just as well. Use your own discretion in this situation.

If you want to be rid of the energy and send it away, you need to find a location that is as far from you as possible. If the spell has a specific target outside yourself or those living with you, you will need to bury the object on the other person's property. Ideally you would have their permission. Please be mindful. Arrests for trespassing are definitely a thing, and that is not the end goal. Keep this—and other common sense—in mind before proceeding.

Types of Dirt

As I mentioned, dirt collected at different places has different energy. An easy way to understand the energy of a specific dirt is to consider what we associate with the location it was taken from. For example, when we think of a bank, we think of money. Therefore, if you're looking to do a prosperity spell, you can use dirt collected at these facilities. Similarly people often visit hospitals to be treated for an affliction they may be suffering from. With this in mind, you can use the dirt collected from hospitals in healing spells. The following list includes common locations and the types of spells their dirt would be useful for. As with all my lists, it is not exhaustive.

Bank: Abundance, money, and prosperity

Courthouse: Justice, legal matters, and truth

Crossroads: Influence, manifestation, and opening doors

Educational facility: Knowledge and studying

Home: Peace, protection, and safety

Hospital: Healing and health

Graveyard: Blessings, protection, and spirit work

Railroad: Drawing toward and sending away

Workplace: Promotions and prosperity

Witchcraft in Action
Happy Home eggshell spell

In the following exercise, we will utilize the act of burying. This spell will have you empty and clean an eggshell to use as the container for the ingredients. At the end of the spell, you will plant it near your home for happiness and protection. The eggshell is dual-purpose, being biodegradable and corresponding with protection.

Materials:
* Egg (for protection)
* Pinch of dried lavender (for peace)
* Pinch of dried rosemary (for protection)
* Pinch of dried cloves (for well-being)
* Pinch of dried chamomile (for prosperity and success)

Directions:
1. Gently crack the egg at the top, making a small hole approximately one-half to one inch wide. Rinse the contents out carefully.
2. Add the lavender to the shell, and give the herb its purpose by stating that it is to bring peace into the lives of those in your home.

3. Add the rosemary, and give the herb its purpose by stating that it is for the protection of the home and those within it.

4. Add the cloves, and give the herb its purpose by stating that it is for the well-being of you and those living with you.

5. Add the chamomile, and give the herb its purpose by stating that it is for successful endeavors and prosperity.

6. Once all of the ingredients are in the eggshell, bury it near your front door. If this isn't in the cards for you, you can bury it in your backyard or a houseplant.

air magick in action

We are in a constant dance with air as it not only surrounds us but occupies space in our bodies. While we can't see it, we can indeed feel it. I briefly touched on wind and directional uses in chapter 5, but I will continue to explore air magick and how we can bring it into our practice here.

Releasing with Wind

Many spells can be bolstered by being released into the wind. Often, the wind sends the energy toward manifestation. That said, wind can also be used to release what is no longer serving you, so you must be clear on your intentions.

Spells involving wind are aplenty, and one of the simplest comes in the form of wishing on a dandelion. That's right. The childhood act of picking those fluffy white poofs and blowing the seeds into the wind to make a wish can be considered an act of witchcraft. Of course, this simple act becomes more potent with more focused intentions. If you happen to come across one of those delightful balls of fluff, lean into the nostalgia and practice this act of manifesting.

As stated, you can also use wind to let go of things and send them away from you. Simply step outdoors and envision the wind carrying away your negative thoughts or stagnant energies.

Types of Winds

Just as each wind's direction carries a particular energy, so does the form of the wind. We can use these subtle energetic differences to assist us in various types of spellwork. Of course, some types of wind will occur more frequently in certain geographic locations, but these differences are good to keep in mind when planning spells and rituals.

Breath: Energy, release, and vitality

Breeze: Anti-anxiety, cleansing, and healing

Cold winds: Banishing, transformation, and vigilance

Damp winds: Nurturing, protection, and purification

Dry winds: Perseverance, strength, and swiftness

Gusts: Change, release, and speed

Storm winds: Power, protection, and strength

Warm winds: Intensity, passion, and warmth

Witchcraft in Action
Letting go spell

As I mentioned, one of the most important things when working with wind is setting an intention. I like to write down my intentions, and they're often to release something or to draw it toward me. For this spell, I will focus on banishing, but it could easily be adapted to manifestation.

Materials:
* Pen or pencil
* Piece of paper
* Firesafe dish
* Lighter or matches
* Breezy or windy day

Directions:
1. Use the pen or pencil to write down what you want to let go of on the piece of paper. It could be a person, feeling, or bad habit. Be specific with your wording.

2. Use the lighter or matches to burn the paper to ashes in the firesafe dish.

3. Allow the ashes to cool. Once cooled, collect the ashes and take them outside.

4. While outside, focus on what you want to let go of as you pay attention to the sensation of the wind blowing.

5. Allow the wind to sweep the ashes away from you as you envision releasing what is no longer yours to hold.

fire magick in action

Think about the element of fire. It is powerful; it is transformative. When using fire in spellwork, we embody these characteristics. Fire is pure energy and holds within it properties of change, beginnings, protection, courage, willpower, and passion. With these associations, it is easy to see why fire is a popular method to use in spellwork. Fire creates a gusto! Sheer energy is transmitted into our working, and it sets transformation into motion.

While physically touching fire is not typically recommended, it is simple enough to safely bring the element into your practice. The size of the fire doesn't matter, so it can be as large or as small as you have the space for.

Burning

Candle magick is popular way to get in touch with this element, but another common way to utilize fire is by burning an object. Burning is a symbol of both activation and cleansing. In many spells, you can use this in place of burying, but as with burying, there are caveats to be mindful of. The first thing to consider is the material that you are burning. Is there cause for concern? Particular objects have chemicals that could have adverse effects when ignited, so you should be mindful of what it's made of or has been treated with. Be that as it may, there are often times when burning an object is more environmentally friendly than burying it. Consider these aspects—and safety in general—when deciding whether to go this route. You will often need tools, such as tweezers or tongs, to create a distance between you and the fire, and you will need to be sure you are working on a fire-safe surface, such as concrete.

Burning, much like utilizing wind, can be used for different goals. When focusing on fire's transformative properties, you can use fire to incite change. If you want to set something in motion, burn an item symbolic of such. If you want to remove something from your life, focus on fire's properties of destruction and burn an object related to what you want to get rid of. If going this route, dispose of the ashes as far away from you as you can manage. You want nothing to do with this anymore.

Types of Fire

Just as different types of dirt and wind have their own correspondences, each type of fire has its own energy as well. Please be mindful of your safety when using any sort of fire in your practice.

Candle: Clarity, passion, and purification

Hearth: Inspiration, prosperity, and protection

Campfire: Nourishment, security, and warmth

Bonfire: Banishing, power, and strength

Wildfire: Banishing, destruction, and intensity

Witchcraft in Action
Bay Leaf manifestation

In my own practice, I frequently burn bay leaves as an act of manifestation, either drawing something toward me or sending something away. This exercise will show you specifically how to use bay leaves to manifest desires.

Materials:
* One bay leaf for each desire
* Permanent marker
* Tweezer or tongs
* Firesafe dish
* Lighter or matches

Directions:
1. Use the marker to down what you want to attract on the bay leaf. Be as specific as possible with the space available.

2. If you have more than one desire, add another bay leaf and write the desire on it. You can add as many or as few bay leaves and intentions as you would like, but keep in mind spellwork requires energy and focus.

3. Once your desire or desires are written, clutch one bay leaf with the tweezers or tongs. Keep the leaf's intention in your mind's eye. Stay focused.

4. Hold the leaf above the firesafe dish, and light it on fire. As the leaf burns, recite what you wrote on it.

5. Repeat steps 3 and 4 with each bay leaf.

6. Take the time to not only envision your words but experience the gratitude of knowing your manifestations are on their way.

7. If you would like, you can take these ashes outdoors and allow the wind to carry them away or gently blow on them to distribute your wishes to the universe.

water magick in action

Water, all metaphysical properties aside, is a very tangible element. We consume water. We bathe and take leisurely swims in water. Our own bodies even consist of up to roughly 60 percent water.[36] Much like air, this is an element that we are in constant contact with. That said, what makes the mundane magickal is the intention.

Water can have many uses within a person's practice. Water has correspondences of healing, purification, and cleansing while also being an element of both emotion and passion. Anyone who has stared down an angry sea in the midst of a storm or had a run-in with rip currents or rapids knows that water is a force to be reckoned with. It is as powerful as it is potent.

Drinking or Consuming

With the growth in popularity of moon water, we are seeing many witches use it as a drink when they need to embody certain characteristics. Need to be more mentally alert and quick-witted? Moon water charged under an air sign would

---

36. Water Science School, "The Water in You."

provide this. Each moon phase, as well as the sign the moon is in, gives the water certain correspondences, and making moon water is quite simple. Just leave water out in the moonlight overnight in an airtight jar and bring it in before sunrise. Moon water can be consumed as normal drinking water or used to make coffee, tea, and soup.

Disposing of in Water

While moon water is having a moment right now, there is also the ritual act of using water as a method of disposal or dispersion, and using a body of water as a symbolic act of removal is commonplace. Simply find a stream or a body of water with a current and use it to carry the spellwork away from you. That said, when using this method, make sure any contents you put in the water are of the earth and biodegradable; they should not affect the environment or any water systems adversely.

Types of Water in Witchcraft

There are many different kinds of water, and their energy will vary. For example, water collected in the midst of a raging hurricane has a different energy and different correspondences than water collected from a calm river or pond. Learn about different types and collect it for spellwork, baths, or consumption. As water is an element of purification and cleansing, you can also gather water to bless and cleanse items. That all being said, please keep safety in mind when collecting water. Take care in hazardous conditions or in situations when the water is meant for consumption, as even rainwater contains pollutants. Proper filtration will be necessary for most water before it is consumed.

Hurricane water: Justice, power, and rapid change

Lake or pond water: Reflection, relaxation, and serenity

Ocean water: Change, force, and power

Rainwater: Blessing, cleansing, and prosperity

River water: Action, change, and motion

Snow water: Creativity, purification, and transformation

Spring water: Purity and renewal

Storm water: Power, protection, and strength

Swamp water: Baneful work, banishing, and binding

Waterfalls: Abundance, power, and rejuvenation

Well water: Healing, manifestations, and purity

Witchcraft in Action
INTUITION tea BLEND

This tea blend can be used to enhance your intuition or even to assist you in achieving prophetic dreams. Remember that black tea is caffeinated, but you can substitute it with white tea, which is lower in caffeine, or forgo it altogether. Please note that mugwort is not safe for individuals who are pregnant or breastfeeding. Lavender can be a substitute for mugwort if necessary.

Materials:
  * 2 teaspoons black tea
  * 1 teaspoon dried mugwort or lavender (to increase your intuition)
  * Pinch of cinnamon (to enhance psychic awareness)
  * Tea infuser or strainer
  * Mug
  * 2 cups water
  * Kettle

Directions:
  1. Bring the water to a boil in the kettle.
  2. Combine the tea and mugwort in the tea infuser or strainer.
  3. Add your tea blend to the mug and pour in hot water.
  4. Allow the ingredients to steep for ten to fifteen minutes.
  5. Add cinnamon to taste, as flavors such as mugwort can be pretty bitter.

Broom Closet Witch Tips

As I mentioned in the previous chapter, there is no better or more discrete way to honor the elements than to simply get outdoors. This is one of the easiest methods to connect with the elements. That said, many of the elements can be felt indoors as well, so your location won't impede your ability to put your practice into action privately.

For instance, with the element of earth, we can spend time outside, but we can also prune or otherwise tend to indoor plants to ground ourselves in nature. Alternatively, we could use their soil to charge items, such as crystals.

We can choose to step outside for fresh air, but we can also open our windows if the weather is nice and invite a cleansing breeze into our home. When smoke cleansing, I like to open doorways to move the energy outward and away from my home.

With the element of fire, we can feel its warmth on a summer day, but we can also bring this element indoors by lighting a candle or a fire in the fireplace. We can use either of these methods to amplify our spellwork.

When it comes to the element of water, we can connect with it by going to a body of water nearby, but we can also utilize the energy by performing a simple cleansing shower or a more elaborate ritual bath in the privacy of our home.

moon magick

If you have spent time on my Instagram account or listening to my podcast, you know that lunar magick plays a fundamental role in my practice. While I firmly believe that if you need to cast a spell promptly, you should do so, I cannot negate the power of working with the lunar cycles. Think of the lunar phases and the signs that they are in as a cosmic oomph that assists your spellwork. While it is not necessary, assuming you utilize other energies in your practice, it can help guide your spellwork and create ease in the work.

In this chapter, I will cover the lunar cycles and the types of magick that are best suited for each phase before getting into Full Moon magick. For each astrological sign, I will include an easy-to-reference list of spellwork best suited to its influences.

Lunar phases

The moon has a long-standing history of being utilized in witchcraft as each phase of the moon can assist a witch's practice in different ways. By understanding what each phase represents, we can align our spellwork and rituals with the stages to lean into their energy. Lunar cycles occur through a 29.5-day span and are broken down into four primary phases: New Moon, Waxing Moon, Full Moon, and Waning Moon. I won't focus on the four secondary phases here, which are Waxing Crescent, Waxing Gibbous, Waning Gibbous, and Waning Crescent, but some practitioners choose to differentiate these subtleties.

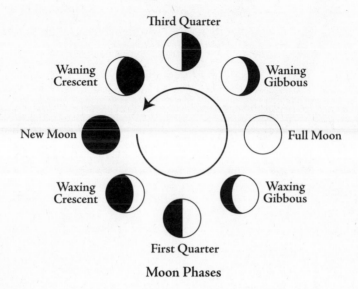

Moon Phases

New Moon

The New Moon occurs when the sun and the moon are aligned. For astrological purposes, this is when both the sun and the moon are in the same sign. When the sun and the moon are perfectly aligned, we witness the phenomenon known as a solar eclipse.

New Moons are barely visible to the naked eye outside of a solar eclipse, and the time when there is no light from the moon and the sky is completely dark is referred to as the Dark Moon. The terms *New Moon* and *Dark Moon* are often used interchangeably, but these two events should be considered separate, if purely for energetic purposes.

During the Dark Moon, the magick best performed is banishing or cursing spellwork, whereas the New Moon is the time to set intentions.

Waxing Moon

With the Dark and New Moons behind us, the Waxing Moon is a period of growth. Slowly the visible portion of the moon becomes larger with each passing day until it reaches its full glory on the Full Moon. During this phase, we should focus on growing the seeds of intentions we set forth during the New Moon. From an energetic standpoint, it is best to view this phase as having an emphasis on our own growth.

The Waxing Moon is also a good time to bring things forward. This could be applied to love, attraction, manifestations, and abundance. We must capitalize on the symbolism of growth and the building of energy and apply them to our workings.

Full Moon

The Full Moon gets the most hype and, subsequently, the most discord. It does not take much to find someone, somewhere, claiming the moon "made me do it," and typically this is said when the moon is flush with energy and at its peak. While the moon is always whole, this is the period when Earth is in between the sun and the moon, and we are able to see the fully illuminated orb from Earth. A lunar eclipse also occurs in this phase, happening when the moon is in Earth's shadow and Earth blocks the sun's light.

The Full Moon is considered the most powerful phase, and it can be used to add an extra jolt of energy into your workings—whatever they may be. While this phase is the strongest, its intensity does not invalidate the purposes of the other lunar phases. If you are a moon water collector, you do not have to wait for a Full Moon to jump into action, but you do need to keep in mind the intentions of each phase.

Waning Moon

The Waning Moon occurs after the Full Moon, and from this point forward, the moon appears to decrease in size until the New Moon arrives. Due to this gradual decrease in size, the Waning Moon is the perfect time for releasing, cleansing, and endings.

The Waning Moon is a period of purging. It is the time to declutter not only your space but your mind and life as well. The waning phase is the time to let go of what is no longer serving you so you can move toward a better path. This phase is the perfect prelude to the intention-setting phase, which occurs directly after it.

fuLL moon magick through the signs

Now that you know that each moon phase has its own correspondences, it's time to focus specifically on the Full Moon and its magick as it relates to astrology. Keep in mind that you can also use astrological correspondences during any moon phase, not just the Full Moon. For instance, Scorpio is an intense and powerful sign, and you can utilize its power during the Full Moon to assist in manifestation. That said, Scorpio energy is also excellent for banishing, just like the energy of a Waning Moon. For a double shot of power, you can utilize a Waning Moon in Scorpio for any banishing magick you need to perform.

Full Moon in Aries

The Aries Full Moon occurs when the sun is in Libra. Aries is the first sign of the zodiac, and when the Full Moon enters Aries, it is a time of beginnings. The Full Moon in Aries can produce a dynamic approach to life and encourage us to dive into things head-on. This sign is certainly not one to shy away from confrontation, so tread lightly when it comes to personal relationships or relationships with those in authority. Your boss likely isn't going to take "the moon made me do it" as a valid excuse for letting them know *exactly* how you feel about them. That said, you can put this dynamic energy to use in your magick—without a doubt.

This influence is great for getting things knocked out and for overcoming obstacles. If you have your eye on the prize, this influence will help you go after it. Utilize this self-starting energy for spellwork involving motivation, be it spell jars or candle spells, and use this time to start projects you have been putting off, be it updating your Book of Shadows or getting outdoors and getting some much-needed vitamin D—weather permitting, of course. With all this energy pulsating about, moon water made during this phase is excellent for spellwork involving positivity and motivation. However, it's also beneficial to save this water to charge items—or yourself—in the future.

Aries Moon Activities

+ Casting spells for motivation
+ Focusing on overcoming obstacles
+ Focusing on yourself
+ Making moon water for charging and positivity
+ Performing spellwork for protection and vitality
+ Trying new ventures

Full Moon in Taurus

The Full Moon in Taurus occurs when the sun is in Scorpio. The Full Moon in Taurus will be a time with underlying stable energy. The sign is known for its sensual nature and being a creature of great comfort, pleasure, and beauty. Due to this, satiating our senses can become the utmost under this influence as will the need for financial stability and security.

This Full Moon can be a time of great sensuality and basking in the beauty life offers. With Taurus's energy being that of stability, this is also a perfect time to work on solidifying your foundation. Spells focusing on stability would do exceptionally well during this time as they will capitalize on the already present energy. This moon ushers in an energy of abundance and makes for a particularly good time to work on manifestations. Due to Taurus's love of the finer things in life, this is also a great time to focus on practicing magick related to prosperity. If you are a Green Witch or just a person who enjoys gardening, this would be a wonderful time to harvest your herbs and save them for future spellwork.

Taurus Moon Activities

- ✦ Charging your crystals
- ✦ Focusing on foundations and stability
- ✦ Harvesting herbs
- ✦ Making moon water for grounding
- ✦ Performing spellwork involving financial growth
- ✦ Planning banishing to perform in the waning phase

Full Moon in Gemini

The Full Moon in Gemini occurs when the sun is in Sagittarius. This influence is a multifaceted one, and we may find ourselves needing to be more mentally stimulated than usual as the sign has a propensity to bore easy. The sign of Gemini is not one to be stifled, and this characteristic can assist us in breaking down barriers and formulating new ideas, making it a good time to start that manuscript or work on that speech you've been putting off. The Full Moon in Gemini is also a good time to focus on your friendships and relationships.

Alternatively, the Full Moon in Gemini could be an optimal time to branch out to make new connections as this is a time for new beginnings. The Full Moon in Gemini will emphasize communication and learning. Due to this emphasis, it would be a good time to journal or practice automatic writing. Simply clear your mind of anticipation, and let words flow freely to you without restraint. The Full

Moon in Gemini would also be a good time to do work regarding communication with your guides, spirits, or deities. Work with your divination tools and open yourself to receiving information. Gemini, being a mental sign and one of learning, makes this a good time to delve further into your practices. Is there something you've been called to learn? Now is the time to do your research and expand your knowledge.

Gemini Moon Activities
◆ Casting spells involving communication
◆ Casting spells involving education and learning
◆ Charging your crystals
◆ Communicating with ancestors
◆ Communicating with spirits, guides, or deities
◆ Making moon water for expanding knowledge
◆ Automatic writing or journaling

Full Moon in Cancer

The Full Moon in Cancer occurs when the sun is in Capricorn. This influence can push things into motion, but it is also one of intuition and introspection, and this watery energy may increase your intuition and your need for solitude during this time. However, do not shy away from the introspective nature of this transit. Allow yourself to connect with your inner world and your inner self to dig into what is taking place inside of you. Developing an understanding of yourself is paramount to success in witchcraft and excelling in the human experience as a whole.

The Full Moon in Cancer is an optimal time to practice magick regarding drawing positive vibes into your abode and yourself. Try making some self-love spell jars or a good vibe home spell to tap into these energies. Water signs are known for their intuition, and because of this, it's a good time to practice divination or explore your intuition through other means, such as meditation or connecting with your third eye. Thanks to this influence's emotional and introspective nature, practicing self-care can be particularly vital. Draw yourself a ritual bath to release any stagnant energy and focus on your intentions while taking care of your external shell. As this influence can be an emotional time, it would be a good time to lean into gratitude journaling to keep your mind focused on the positives and to keep your vibration elevated.

Cancer Moon Activities
+ Charging your crystals
+ Creating a good vibes spell for your home
+ Creating a gratitude list to stay positive
+ Making moon water for love and protection
+ Taking ritual baths
+ Utilizing divination to tap into your increased intuition

Full Moon in Leo

The Full Moon in Leo occurs when the sun is in Aquarius. Leo is a charismatic sign that has no issue reveling in the spotlight. In fact, the sign prefers it. This energy is a showstopper that has no issue being bold and taking up space. If you tend to be introverted or shy, the Full Moon in Leo could be a period when you do not mind taking up some of the spotlight. This influence makes it a good time to focus on creative ventures and learning how to take up space for yourself. Do not be afraid to advocate for yourself during this time. It is okay to be your own biggest fan. You must cheer for yourself first, then the rest will follow.

The influence of Leo makes it a particularly powerful time for manifestation. With energies high, this transit is a great time for most magick. The sign's extra vote of confidence raises your vibration, and you can align more easily with your goals without the added weight of self-doubt. With the fire element present in this Full Moon, it's also a particularly good time for candle magick, especially if the intent is career or creativity focused. If you have kept any creative pursuits tucked away in your back pocket, now is the time to bring them to the forefront. Feel free to charge your crystals and moon water to harvest some of this creative, courageous energy.

Leo Moon Activities
+ Being adventurous
+ Casting self-confidence spells
+ Making moon water for confident energy

- Performing candle magick
- Performing magick focused on career, confidence, and creativity
- Sending out powerful manifestations

Full Moon in Virgo

The Full Moon in Virgo occurs when the sun is in Pisces. The Virgo influence produces a meticulous energy and an emphasis on health, career, and routines. If you find yourself creating to-do lists, organizing the chaos, or cleaning out clutter that has accumulated over your lifetime, lean into it. Decluttering your space has been proven to positively affect your mental health and well-being. Get your donation bags ready. It is time to cleanse your space.

The Full Moon's heightened powers and Virgo's influence make this a particularly good time to practice magick involving your career, to introduce new wellness habits, or to perform magick involving health and productivity. With the emphasis on order and cleanliness, this would be a good time to craft protection and banishing sprays and protective floor washes for your home. Floor washes can be simple to make, and they're an easy way to combine magick with the mundane. Simply add herbs that align with your intentions to your chosen liquid. This liquid could be water from the faucet, moon water made under this phase, or vinegar. This is an excellent use of the moon, but if you are sensitive to lunar phases and find yourself exhausted, you can simply make moon water for any future work that requires a meticulous nature.

Virgo Moon Activities

- Creating banishing sprays
- Creating health spells and amulets
- Creating magickal floor washes
- Making moon water for planning and meticulousness
- Performing productivity magick
- Performing spellwork involving careers
- Setting intentions for health and career

Full Moon in Libra

The Full Moon in Libra occurs when the sun is in Aries. The influence of Libra is very charming and social with an emphasis on aesthetics. Libra lives and breathes balance. Due to this, Libra is a natural diplomat and a sign of righteousness and fairness. With that social element and eye for beauty playing together in cohesion, the Full Moon in Libra will be focused more on partnerships—both romantic and platonic.

A Full Moon in Libra would be a good time to plant the seeds of attraction, self-love, and companionship. If you want to attract new friendships or a potential partner, this would be a great moon to do this under. Venus rules Libra, so use this to your advantage in your cosmic workings. This influence of a just nature also makes it an opportune time to focus on spellwork regarding legal matters as well as justice as a whole. If you are looking to sway a legal case in your favor, this is a good influence to do just that. The Full Moon in Libra can be a wonderful influence for recalibrating ourselves, and spellwork relating to finding our balance and inner peace can be particularly successful. You may also choose to make moon water during this time for work related to beauty, partnerships, justice, or balance.

Libra Moon Activities

+ Casting spells for career success
+ Doing work involving relationships
+ Making moon water for balance, beauty, justice, or partnerships
+ Performing attraction magick
+ Performing spellwork involving legal matters
+ Setting intentions for inner peace and self-love

Full Moon in Scorpio

The Full Moon in Scorpio takes place when the sun is in Taurus. Scorpio is a powerful water sign known for its intuition, determination, and sexuality, and this can be a period of intensity. While Scorpio is a water sign, its energy can bring the heat and even the sting if necessary. The Full Moon in Scorpio can assist you in surmounting any obstacles in your way and seeing goals to fruition.

Scorpio Full Moons are useful for adding an extra oomph to your magickal workings in general. This cosmic influence will carry the prowess that Scorpio is known for, making it a good time for spells involving overcoming hurdles and facing fears. This Full Moon is a great time for self-empowerment work and self-improvement. This influence is also one of passion, which makes this time excellent for performing boudoir magick and the like. Do you have something you need to remove from your life or let go of? Good. This influence is a wonderful time for banishing work as well as personal transformations. The sign of Scorpio is known to close doors on those who betray them, so you can utilize this type of steadfast decision-making to help you remove people or circumstances that are no longer serving you.

Scorpio Moon Activities

+ Casting spells for transformation
+ Facing fears and overcoming obstacles
+ Making moon water for psychic energy and power
+ Performing banishing and protective magick
+ Performing magick for self-empowerment and self-improvement
+ Performing sex magick

Full Moon in Sagittarius

The Full Moon in Sagittarius occurs when the sun is in Gemini. Be mindful of your word choice during this influence as Sagittarius does not mince words. This energy is known to be one of travel and philosophy as well as one of high stamina and a sharp tongue. This adventurous spirit may take you in directions you otherwise might not have. Lean into it. The Sagittarius Full Moon is an optimistic influence, so make the best of its cosmic leverage as you enter this new cycle.

When the Full Moon enters Sagittarius, it is entering a sign of expansion. You may find that you are more eager to learn; allow yourself to tap into this. If you need to cast a spell to help you focus on school or learn a subject, this would be an ideal time to do so. With all that free-spirited energy cycling about, it is time to bottle it up. You know what I am talking about, witches. That's right—moon water. Due to the nature of this sign, spellwork involving safe travels and optimism will also be particularly potent, but do not limit yourself to just spellwork and rituals. Use this energy and moon phase to clarify your goals and intentions. If you already have a goal in mind, use this energy to explore its terrain further.

Sagittarius Moon Activities

- Casting spells for safe travels and education
- Exploring new ideas and opportunities
- Making moon water for transformation
- Performing spellwork involving positive energy and happiness
- Utilizing adventurous energy and being spontaneous
- Working toward your goals

Full Moon in Capricorn

The Full Moon in Capricorn occurs when the sun is in Cancer. When the moon enters Capricorn, it brings forth a studious and tenacious energy that will assist you in knuckling down and taking care of business. This cosmic boost could provide you with the professional motivation to achieve the goals you have set your sights on and to see projects through to completion.

This Full Moon brings an energy of seriousness, determination, and stability, and when the moon enters Capricorn, it is a good time for power, manifesting goals, and financial stability. If you have been waiting to perform magick centered on your career path or life trajectory, this would be an optimal time to do so. Maybe you feel like you lack the motivation and overall focus to accomplish what you need to do. For this, make some moon water, pour it into your coffee maker, and brew coffee with it for an extra jolt of productivity when you are in need. Moon water made during this time will assist with determination, productivity, and matters related to careers. This sign is known to hold on to things like vision—and grudges. Use this laser focus to do binding work or other work you need to have a long-lasting effect.

Capricorn Moon Activities

- Casting spells for success
- Charging items to cultivate hardworking energy
- Making moon water for productivity and power
- Making professional moves
- Performing binding work
- Performing manifestation work

Full Moon in Aquarius

The Full Moon enters Aquarius when the sun is in Leo, and Aquarius brings an analytical and independent vibe that will take you to a new cerebral level and chip away at any stigmas that may be holding you back. This energy marches to the beat of its own drummer, so use this time to do the same. Feel weird? Good. Throw conformity to the wayside and embrace your inner weirdo for a bit; life is better that way. Use this cosmic boost to stimulate creativity and stretch your imagination beyond its normal confines; it is a wonderful time to think outside of the box.

The Aquarius influence is one of truth-seeking. Therefore, when the Full Moon enters Aquarius, it is a good time to review your truth or practice divination that focuses on uncovering hidden truths. It is also a wonderful time to have creative visions and envision the future you'd like for yourself. Aquarius is a big-picture sign, so utilize this time to create a vision board and think of a future that is not limited by societal normalcy. This progressive influence makes this a good time to focus on spells involving future success and self-expression. Thanks to the cerebral nature of this sign, emotions are not as high as they can be during other Full Moons as it balances the energy of heightened emotions with detachment. Moon water made during this time will have innovative and adventurous energy.

Aquarius Moon Activities

+ Casting spells involving expression and truths
+ Charging items to cultivate inventive energies
+ Creating a vision board
+ Making moon water for innovation and expression
+ Performing divination for hidden truths
+ Performing success spells

Full Moon in Pisces

The Full Moon in Pisces occurs when the sun is in Virgo. When the moon is in Pisces, you can expect this influence to stimulate your imagination and increase your intuition. This moon also provides an energy that assists and facilitates change. Use this influence to fully explore what needs maintenance and what can be let go of. Focus on the areas of your life that need your energy versus areas that are simply not worth your time and act accordingly.

This sign represents the subconscious, so when the Full Moon enters this sign, it is a particularly good time to explore the world of dreams, working with both lucid and prophetic dreams. The most important part to this process is remembering to record the dreams you have. The best way to do this is to record them immediately upon waking so you can dissect their meanings and symbolism later. If you have not tried astral projection, this may be an opportune time to start practicing. This Full Moon lends itself to enhanced daydreaming, intuitiveness, and empathy, and you can work with these qualities to strengthen your creativity during this time and release any blockages that may inhibit you from moving forward. Set out your moon water and crystals to charge them under this influence. They will become useful for divination, psychic development, creativity, imagination, and release.

Pisces Moon Activities

+ Charging items to cultivate imaginative energy
+ Creating a dream journal
+ Making moon water for psychic energy
+ Performing divination
+ Performing spells involving psychic enhancement
+ Practicing astral projection

Broom Closet Witch Tips

The good news is that observing lunar cycles can be a very discreet way to connect with your craft. While more elaborate rituals might raise flags, simple rituals, such as placing moon water and crystals on your windowsill for charging, can go largely undetected. There are apps that can help you see what phase and sign the moon is in, and many of them are free. If an app isn't an option or not available, a quick query on your preferred search engine will provide you with the information you are after.

As I've mentioned, meditation is a great way to connect with your craft, and it is also a practice that is not inherently "witchy." Making time to gaze at the moon or watch the sunset and the moonrise should not arouse any suspicion, and while you *should* meditate more often than just on the Full or New Moons, you can use these times to perform meditation rituals that honor the lunar cycles.

Another discrete method, which I recommend doing whether you're in the broom closet or not, is keeping a journal of the energy you feel during the different cycles. This will help you start to determine how particular lunar phases, as well as their astrological correspondences, affect you personally. This practice will give you insight into your connection with the cosmos, and it can assist you in determining the best ways to honor your own responses to the cycles.

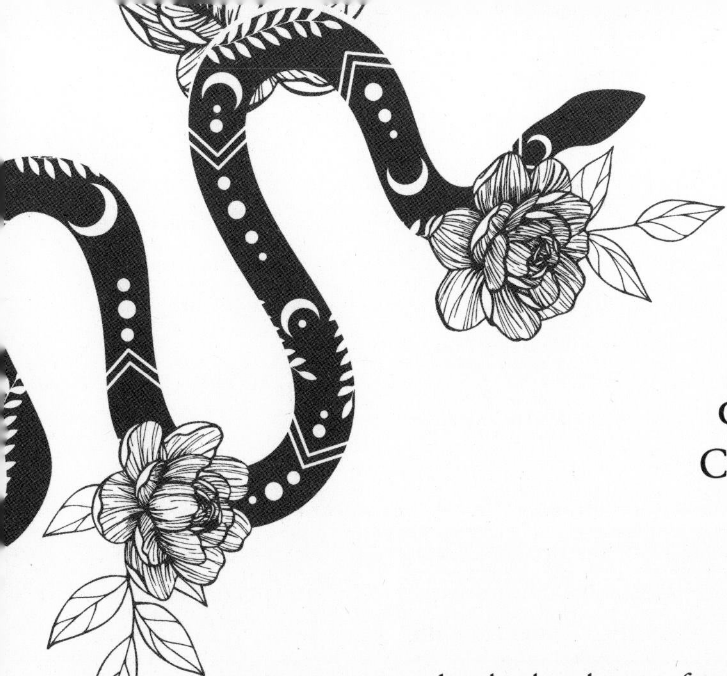

Chapter Eight
Crystals

It is easy to marvel at the sheer beauty of crystals. The way they glimmer, shine, and flash is captivating, to say the least. However, beyond their visual appeal lies the energy residing inside them. Each crystal's energetic correspondences are as unique as the individual crystals themselves. Although I have always been enamored with crystals' aesthetics, the energy they house has become an invaluable part of my practice; crystals are powerful allies.

My connection to crystals and the earth came at a very early age. Though, at the time, it was an organic interest versus an intentional practice. In my childhood, I quickly replied with "rocks" whenever anyone would ask what I'd like to have as a travel souvenir, and frankly, my present-day response to that question is perilously close to the same. The gifts I received were not purchased. Instead, friends and family gathered them from trails or streams along their journeys, making them all the more valuable to a young gem enthusiast like myself.

In modern times, there has been a rise in both crystal collectors and crystal resellers. While the availability of crystals and other such specimens has increased, it is not without its downside. Questions about ethical sourcing have emerged—and for a good reason. Often, the locations where many crystals are mined cut costs by utilizing child labor, unfair wages, and unsafe working conditions, and the low cost of crystals can potentially indicate that these methods, or variations of them, are in use. It is wise to be wary of sellers who seem evasive or are unable to give clear answers about where their crystals are sourced.

Although I will cover cleansing in this chapter, it is best if we are mindful of where our crystals originated from in order to ensure that ethical practices are afoot. Making a conscious effort to care for both our planet and its inhabitants should be of utmost importance—not only as witches but as human beings. Whenever possible, it is best to use what you have on hand.

CLEANSING

When we first purchase our crystals, or even after our own personal usage, the crystals need to be cleansed. Cleansing dispels any negative energy the crystals may be holding on to and helps return the crystals to their original state.

Think about yourself. After hanging around low-vibe energies or toxic people, you need to cleanse your spirit and aura from the cosmic drainage. Crystals work in a similar fashion. Yes, crystals carry their own frequencies, but they can also absorb energies, and once a crystal has absorbed energy, it holds on to it until it is properly cleansed.

How will you know when your crystals need to be cleansed? For starters, you should cleanse your crystals when you purchase them. Most crystals probably traveled a great distance before they arrived to you. The energy they gathered along the way may not align with you, and they should be cleansed accordingly.

Method One: Water

You can cleanse your crystals in a dish of water or under running water. Keep your crystals submerged for approximately one minute to cleanse them of unnecessary energies.

Remember that not all crystals are water safe!

Certain crystals can become tarnished or degraded by being submerged in liquid for a prolonged period. To know if a crystal can withstand being submerged, you must take into account the Mohs hardness scale, which measures the hardness of minerals—but it isn't the entire scope. While it is often stated that crystals above a five on the Mohs scale can be submerged in water, some crystals will rust. Crystals that can deteriorate in water include pyrite, hematite, and magnetite. Generally, the quartz family is considered water safe, but tangerine quartz isn't due to the iron oxide in the composition of the crystal.

Crystals That Are Not Water Safe[37]

- Amber
- Ammolite
- Angelite
- Apatite
- Apophyllite
- Azurite
- Calcite
- Celestite
- Fire opal
- Fluorite
- Gypsum
- Halite (rock salt)
- Hematite
- Kunzite
- Kyanite
- Lepidolite
- Malachite
- Moonstone
- Pyrite
- Red coral
- Rhodochrosite
- Selenite
- Tangerine quartz
- Turquoise
- Ulexite

Method Two: Salt

This method is also simple and effective. Pour Himalayan salt into a dish, filling it approximately three-quarters of the way full, and place your crystals in the salt. Leave your crystals there for at least twenty-four hours for a proper cleanse.

Specific crystals can also become damaged if placed in salt for a prolonged period as it can fade pigmented stones. While faded stones are not less powerful, they are less aesthetically pleasing and salt can deteriorate the stone over time.

Method Three: Smoke Cleansing

Another method that you can use is smoke cleansing. For this method, you can use an herb bundle or incense to cleanse the crystals. Once you have chosen which of these to use, light the end and wait for the smoke to billow. While holding the crystal, surround it with the smoke for approximately one minute to clear out the adverse energy.

---

37. "The Mohs Hardness Scale and Chart for Select Gems," International Gem Society.

Method Four: Selenite

Selenite is a self-cleansing, purifying crystal, and it is also helpful in cleansing other crystals. To accomplish this, you must tie or place selenite on the crystal you intend to cleanse. When I use this technique, I leave it on the crystal for approximately twenty-four hours.

Method Five: Sunlight/Moonlight

Using the sun or moon's light is another perfect, simple method for both cleansing and recharging your crystals. When using either of them for cleansing, leave your crystal on a windowsill or outdoors for the duration of the day or night. However, be wary of placing quartz under direct sunlight. It has the potential to become a fire hazard. Ever use a magnifying glass to start a fire? Yes—it's just like that.

CHARGING

Charging your crystals is also necessary. This step should follow cleansing your crystals for the best result, though several of the methods listed are dual-purpose and accomplish both.

Some crystals disperse their energy onto the recipient, and others absorb energy. Therefore, both cleansing and charging are pertinent for your own crystal babies. A good comparison is to think of your crystal as a battery. After a time, your crystal, just like a battery, will need to be recharged.

Don't know if your crystal needs to be charged? Don't be afraid to use your intuition. Do you feel that its energy has decreased, is clouded, or is otherwise not as vibrant as it once was? If so, it's time. However, a good rule of thumb is to cleanse and charge your crystals once a month to every few months to keep them at their best.

Method One: Sunlight

Sunlight is a dual-purpose method that can be used to charge your crystals via solar power. As mentioned earlier in the cleansing portion of this article, be careful with clear quartz as it can be a fire hazard.

Method Two: Moonlight

Crystals can also be charged under the moonlight. This is a more delicate process than sunlight and is also dual-purpose. To do so, place your crystal in the moonlight in a safe location. Many times, the perfect place is on the windowsill. Leave the crystal in the moonlight until the following day. You can charge crystals under any moon phase, but the Full Moon is particularly powerful for charging your crystals as it is most potent.

Method Three: Intention

You can charge your stones by meditating with them and visualizing your intentions. This method is a great way to bond with your crystals and program them with your intent. To use this method, you must hold the crystal in your palm while focusing on your intention. Do this until you feel that the energy has shifted into the stone, charging the crystal with its purpose.

Method Four: Crystal Grids

A crystal grid is not just something nice to look at, although, admittedly, it is. Rather, a crystal grid is an intentional alignment of crystals rooted in sacred geometry used for a specific purpose. As such, this method can be used for charging. To accomplish this, place the focal crystal in the center of the grid and surround it with smaller crystals such as quartz or selenite. Once the crystals are situated, leave the grid in place for at least a day.

Method Five: Other Stones

There are a handful of crystals that naturally replenish energies. For example, you can place an amethyst or citrine near the stone you want to charge and *voila!* You have a crystal-to-crystal recharge.

USING CRYSTALS

Crystals can serve several purposes, and some of these include using them during meditation, placing them on your altar, using them in spellwork, and wearing jewelry made with them. Each of these uses can be personalized however you see fit, and I will give you a general idea of how to use them in the following paragraphs.

Even those who do not utilize crystals in their daily practice would likely agree that they're beautiful, and wearing crystals can be both fashionable and mindful. Need help deciding which crystals to wear? Review the quick reference list following this section to find out which crystals are best suited for the qualities you wish to attract or embody in your own life. Next, you will need to sit with your crystal and assign it its purpose. While a stone may carry a specific frequency that aligns with an intention, you need to connect with your crystal and energetically give it an objective. This can be done through meditation, and crystals themselves can actually assist you in meditation.

Meditation with crystals can be done by surrounding yourself with crystals, or you can even place the crystals on top of you. Some practitioners will also use specific stones and put them on each chakra point. This is not a large part of my practice, but it is something you can easily dig into further if it's of interest to you.

Crystal chips are small fragments of a crystal, and they're useful for small sachets or spell jars. When it comes to these tiny crystals, you can either order them that size or make your own by chipping away at a more significant piece with a heavy object, such as a hammer. If this is in your wheelhouse, make sure to take appropriate precautions. Wear safety glasses, gloves, and proper garments for the occasion. As someone who has managed to stab herself with crystal shards on more than one occasion, take my word for it—you do not want those pieces in or around your cornea. If you are the type that needs to make a mistake for yourself, by all means, go ahead, but do not say I did not warn you.

Crystals can also make great additions to your altar. Not only are they aesthetically pleasing, but you can work in unison with their energetic properties. Crystals also make a suitable representation of earth when creating an elemental altar. However, there are several different types of altars where crystals have a place, and depending on space and preference, you may have more than one of them in your home. It is also a common custom to use a crystal altar for meditative practices.

And if none of these fit your vibe, you can always carry a crystal in your pocket in a pinch. Or your bra, if you wear one—no judgment.

One of my favorite crystal reference books is *The Crystal Bible* by Judy Hall. Most of my notes over the years have been collected from the pages of her books, and, as such, they were a vital resource in compiling this list.

QUICK CRYSTAL REFERENCE[38]

Abundance: Bloodstone, carnelian, cinnabar, citrine, dendritic agate, diamond, fluorite, hawk's-eye, jade, malachite, moss agate, ruby, tiger's-eye, and topaz

Anxiety: Amethyst, apophyllite, beryl, cerussite, chrysoprase, hematite, jasper, kunzite, rhodonite, and rutilated quartz

Attraction: Rhodochrosite and rose quartz

Beauty: Dioptase, opal, and ruby

Business: Carnelian, cerussite, chrysoprase, cinnabar, citrine, clear quartz, diamond, fire opal, garnet, jet, pyrite, and yellow tourmaline

Calming: Agate, apophyllite, aquamarine, azeztulite, blue lace agate, cerussite, citrine, fire agate, hawk's-eye, howlite, selenite, and snowflake obsidian

Communication: Amazonite, angelite, apatite, aquamarine, blue obsidian, celestite, chrysocolla, dendritic chalcedony, larimar, moldavite, moss agate, smoky quartz, and sugilite

Creativity: Alexandrite, ametrine, apatite, aventurine, bloodstone, Botswana agate, carnelian, cerussite, citrine, chrysoberyl, chrysocolla, chrysoprase, Herkimer diamond, kunzite, lapis lazuli, larimar, opal, pink chalcedony, pyrite, and ulexite

Decision: Amethyst, azeztulite, green apophyllite, and onyx

Depression: Amazonite, amethyst, angelite, apatite, blue chalcedony, black calcite, Botswana agate, citrine, idocrase, jet, kunzite, lapis lazuli, pyrite, orange calcite, and spessartite

Dreamwork: Alexandrite, amethyst, basanite, bloodstone, blue howlite, celestite, chalcedony, charoite, danburite, elbaite, Herkimer diamond, jade, jasper, kyanite, lapis lazuli, malachite, moonstone, rhodochrosite, ruby, sapphire, and ulexite

Energy work: Agate, amazonite, amber, carnelian, pyrite, tourmaline, and selenite

---

38. Hall, *The Crystal Bible*.

Fatigue: Ametrine, citrine, dioptase, and pyrite

Focus: Lepidolite and sapphire

Forgiveness: Chrysoberyl, chrysoprase, obsidianite, pink calcite, rutilated quartz, rhodonite, sugilite, and topaz

Grief: Amethyst, Apache tear, azurite, dioptase, fire opal, lithium quartz, magnetite, onyx, pink calcite, rainbow aura, rose quartz, and sugilite

Growth: Agate, aquamarine, aventurine, calcite, fuchsite, Herkimer diamond, malachite, moldavite, obsidian, prehnite, rutilated quartz, rhodonite, sapphire, tektite, tourmaline, and unakite

Happiness: Alexandrite, carnelian, cat's-eye, chalcedony, chrysocolla, citrine, larimar, muscovite, opal aura quartz, orange jade, rainbow aura, sardonyx, smithsonite, sunstone, topaz, and yellow jade

Health: Apatite, bloodstone, fuchsite, hessonite, pyrite, red jasper, shattuckite, topaz, tourmaline, and unakite

Independence: Chrysoprase, golden beryl, lepidolite, and sunstone

Inspiration: Angelite, apatite, azeztulite, carnelian, chrysocolla, citrine, emerald, garnet, kunzite, moldavite, moss agate, rhodolite, sulfur, sunstone, and tourmaline

Intuition: Amethyst, alexandrite, apophyllite, aquamarine, azurite, bloodstone, cat's-eye, citrine, fluorite, hessonite, labradorite, magnetite, malachite, Merlinite, moonstone, muscovite, obsidian, pietersite, pyrite, rhodolite, star sapphire, smithsonite, sodalite, spinel, and stilbite

Justice: Amethyst, aventurine, bloodstone, diamond, hematite, jade, jet, lapis lazuli, sapphire, selenite, and tourmaline

Love: Agate, alexandrite, amazonite, amethyst, apophyllite, atacamite, beryl, carnelian, celestite, charoite, chrysocolla, diamond, emerald, garnet, pink calcite, rhodonite, and rose quartz

Luck: Agate, alexandrite, amazonite, aventurine, bloodstone, cat's-eye, citrine, diamond, jade, jasper, jet, lodestone, malachite, obsidian, opal, pearl, sardonyx, smoky quartz, staurolite, sunstone, and tiger's-eye

Manifestation: Amazonite, apatite, alexandrite, chalcedony, citrine, diamond, kyanite, okenite, prehnite, smoky quartz, stilbite, tiger's-eye, topaz, yellow fluorite, and yellow phenacite

Mental clarity: Ametrine, atacamite, brecciated jasper, celestite, chrysocolla, diamond, emerald, lapis lazuli, larimar, obsidian, peridot, selenite, and ulexite

Motivation: Amethyst, apatite, calcite, carnelian, chrysocolla, citrine, red tiger's-eye, and ruby

Patience: Amber, aragonite, bloodstone, danburite, emerald, howlite, jade, jasper, obsidian, and tourmaline

Positivity: Amber, amethyst, azeztulite, beryl, calcite, carnelian, chalcedony, chlorite, chrysoprase, citrine, dioptase, emerald, fuchsite, howlite, magnesite, magnetite, malachite, moss agate, opal, phenacite, pyrite, rhodochrosite, rose quartz, ruby, smoky quartz, spinel, sugilite, sunstone, thulite, Tibetan quartz, tourmalinated quartz, tourmaline, and yellow jasper

Prosperity: Black agate, citrine, fluorite, green aventurine, hawk's-eye, jet, pyrite, ruby, sapphire, and tourmaline

Protection: Amethyst, amazonite, amber, ametrine, angelite, aventurine, azeztulite, bloodstone, carnelian, cat's-eye, chiastolite, diamond, fire agate, fluorite, garnet, jade, jasper, jet, kunzite, lapis lazuli, obsidian, onyx, opal, pyrite, rhodolite, ruby, smoky quartz, and tourmaline

Psychic: Amethyst, ametrine, andradite, angelite, apatite, aventurine, azurite, calcite, chrysocolla, dioptase, emerald, fluorite, hessonite, Herkimer diamond, jet, kyanite, labradorite, lapis lazuli, malachite, moonstone, muscovite, obsidian, opal, and quartz

Relaxation: Apophyllite, calcite, celestite, chalcedony, charoite, chrysoprase, fire agate, grossularite, magnesite, pink tourmaline, smoky quartz, and ulexite

Stress: Amethyst, apophyllite, beryl, cerussite, chrysoprase, hematite, jasper, kunzite, rhodonite, and rutilated quartz

Trust: Amazonite, amber, apophyllite, atacamite, blue lace agate, calcite, carnelian, celestite, chalcedony, charoite, chrysoprase, diamond, kunzite, labradorite, melanite, moss agate, prehnite, rhodolite, rose quartz, and sapphire

Vitality: Amber, aquamarine, bloodstone, calcite, carnelian, cerussite, citrine, fire agate, fluorite, garnet, obsidian, prehnite, pyrope, spinel, sunstone, tiger's-eye, and tourmaline

Willpower: Calcite, hematite, pietersite, and sardonyx

Wisdom: Amber, amethyst, celestite, cerussite, citrine, danburite, emerald, howlite, jade, labradorite, moldavite, pyrope, rhyolite, sapphire, serpentine, snow quartz, staurolite, sugilite, topaz, and tourmaline

Witchcraft in Action
tranquility crystal grid

For this exercise, we will create a crystal grid to inspire tranquility in ourselves and our homes. These grids are typically based on sacred geometry, and if you prefer to follow a pattern, you can buy a cloth with a design to guide you. That isn't necessary, though, and you can simply print off a geometric shape, like a flower of life, or forgo a pattern entirely. If you choose not to use a design, it is easy to create one intuitively.

Materials:
*   *   Large amethyst (for tranquility)
*   *   5 to 8 clear quartz tumbles or points (for amplifying intentions)
*   *   5 to 8 rose quartz tumbles or points (for love)
*   *   Crystal grid or printout of sacred geometric shape (optional)
*   *   Incense or herb bundle for cleansing
*   *   Lighter or matches

Directions:
1. The first step when making any crystal grid is to set your intention. For this exercise, our intention is to foster a loving and peaceful vibration for ourselves and our homes. Keep this in mind for the duration of the practice.
2. Light the herb bundle or incense and use the smoke to cleanse your space and your crystals, removing any unnecessary energy.

While using herb bundles and incense are my favorite methods, you are welcome to use whatever works best for you.

3. If you are using a physical grid or printout, position it in the desired location. If you're not using a grid, that's fine; simply place your crystals intuitively. No matter your method, start by placing the amethyst in the center. The amethyst is the focal stone. Then put the small tumbles around the amethyst. Try to keep the spacing between the crystals consistent.

4. After your crystals are arranged, it is time to activate your grid. As you focus on your intention of tranquility, envision the crystals' energy spidering out to each and every one of the other crystals, working together in unison. Think of this as a web of energy, connecting each stone to the next. Sometimes it's helpful to physically touch objects when you are first starting out, and you may run your fingers along the grid, moving from crystal to crystal, which creates a sacred connection between the crystals.

5. Return your focus to the center crystal and focus on feeding this crystal your energy. At this point in the process, it helps me to build energy by moving. You can dance or otherwise raise your heart rate to build momentum. Once you've built momentum, hold the intention of tranquility in your mind. Place your palms in a cupping position around the amethyst, and envision the energy you have accumulated transferring directly into the amethyst.

6. Once you've completed step 5, the energy has been transmitted into the crystals themselves, and each of the smaller crystals is now working together in a cosmic symbiosis. Personally, I leave my crystal grids up for weeks on end. If I feel as if the energy has shifted, I simply reactivate my grid by repeating steps 4 and 5.

Broom Closet Witch Tips

Crystals are beautiful, and these items can be quickly passed off as home decor with little to no meaning behind them. Crystals are even sold in stores like HomeGoods, so having a crystal in your home will not sound any alarms for the average Joe. As I said, I collected "rocks" long before I was aware of their metaphysical properties, and nobody was the wiser once I discovered their intricacies and the energy they possess.

Crystals are not only a connection to the earth, but depending on the crystal, they can have associations with other elements as well. If crystals are a part of your practice, you can use different types to create a discrete altar that honors each of the elements.

Earth: Agate, black tourmaline, jade, malachite, and tiger's-eye

Air: Amethyst, kyanite, labradorite, lapis lazuli, and sodalite

Fire: Carnelian, citrine, fire agate, red garnet, and sunstone

Water: Aquamarine, chrysoprase, kunzite, moonstone, and opal

Crystals can also be utilized as wards in the form of jewelry or decorations placed in your home, and they can be assigned other purposes as well, such as to attract love and compassion or cultivate intuition.

And that's not all, crystals can be used in meditation and ritual baths discretely as well!

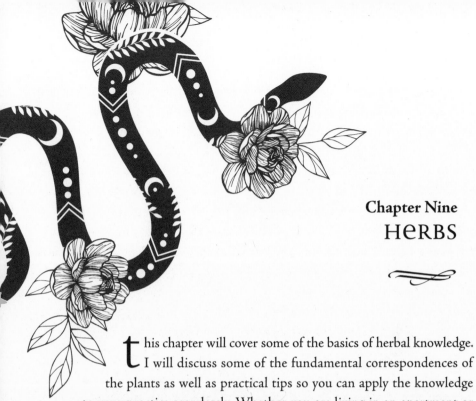

Chapter Nine

HERBS

t his chapter will cover some of the basics of herbal knowledge. I will discuss some of the fundamental correspondences of the plants as well as practical tips so you can apply the knowledge to your practice seamlessly. Whether you are living in an apartment or have a self-proclaimed black thumb, this chapter can assist you in developing a relationship with herbs that works for you.

When we use herbs, we connect with the spirits of the plants and then use their correspondences to enhance our spellwork or rituals. While these herbs can be utilized in a variety of different methods and magickal applications, plants themselves *are* magick. These magnificent beings rise from the earth with their own frequency, and this contributes to making them a perfect pairing to earth-based traditions.

GROWING HERBS

Even if you are not planning on using the plants for spellwork, the act of gardening in itself is a meditative experience, and it allows for a grounding connection to the earth. As I mentioned, plants carry their own frequency. This makes them great purifiers in the home as well as serving a purpose of protection and transmuting negative energy.

Personally, one of my favorite parts of my home and one of my favorite parts of my practice are one and the same: my herb gardens. Yes, plural. While I am in a constant battle with the Florida sun, there are few things that are more pertinent to my magickal practice than growing my own herbs. My yard itself is largely a mixture of sand and sporadic patches of grass, so I utilize the areas available to me, which are two raised beds, and I've lined my walkways with herbs that prefer dryer climates and don't mind that the ground is half sand, half soil.

Many herbs do great in windowsills, or indoors in general, so if you are living in a city or an apartment where actual ground area is hard to come by, you can still grow your own herbs if the practice calls to you. Some of the herbs that grow well indoors include basil, cilantro, chives, parsley, dill, oregano, thyme, mint, rosemary, lavender, and garden sage. Whether you are growing them from seeds or seedlings, the packets or plant tabs will have the proper watering and sunlight instructions for each herb. While it is not exactly necessary for spellwork, growing your own herbs does foster a connection to the plant matter you use from seed to fruition, and this bond can play a pivotal role in your connection to your craft.

BUYING HERBS

Recently there has been a bit of a buzz around "McCormick" traditions. While it is meant in jest, it is also a very convenient starting place, so I am going to review some of the correspondences for popular McCormick herbs and spices. Why not knock out your witchy wares while also completing your grocery shopping? We are in the age of busyness, so streamlining and being resourceful are useful ventures.

"McCormick" Correspondences

Allspice: Luck, money, and prosperity

Basil: Love, peace, prosperity, and protection

Bay leaves: Divination, messengers, protection, and strength

Caraway: Fidelity, health, passion, and protection

Cayenne: Baneful magick, fidelity, hex-breaking, and love

Celery: Psychic enhancement, sexuality, and strength

Chili powder: Baneful magick, fidelity, hex-breaking, and love

Chives: Banishing, health, and protection

Cilantro: Healing, health, and love

Cinnamon: Love, manifestations, sexuality, speed, and success

Cloves: Banishing, love, money, and protection

Cumin: Anti-theft, fidelity, and protection

Curry: Energy, passion, and protection

Dill: Good fortune, love, money, and protection

Fennel: Healing, protection, and purification

Ginger: Prosperity, sexuality, and success

Marjoram: Happiness, health, money, and protection

Mustard: Courage, fertility, protection, and strength

Nutmeg: Health, luck, money, and psychic enhancement

Onion: Banishing, health, prophetic dreams, and protection

Oregano: Creativity, healing, love, and protection

Paprika: Energy and increasing power

Parsley: Inspiration, peace, protection, strength, and wealth

Pepper: Baneful magick, banishing, and protection

Poppy: Invisibility, luck, prosperity, and restful sleep

Rosemary: Banishing, mental clarity, protection, and purification

Sage: Healing, protection, purification, and wisdom

Salt: Protection and purification

Sesame: Good fortune, prosperity, and sexuality

Tarragon: Compassion, love, and protection

Thyme: Courage, healing, psychic enhancement, and restful sleep

Turmeric: Banishing, strength, protection, and vitality

Stocking up on grocery store herbs is an easy way to build your apothecary affordably and practically. Using these herbs also opens the door to kitchen witchery as they are made for consumption and therefore safe to eat.

Nevertheless, purchasing from the grocery store is certainly not the only way to obtain dry herbs. Oftentimes, there will be specialty herbal shops within driving distance. The selection in these locations far surpasses those at the local market. Another option for more obscure herbs is to check out any metaphysical shop in your area as they may also have them available. If you are hesitant to visit any of these locations, for whatever reason, there are several reputable sellers online as well.

DRYING HERBS

There are a few methods that you can use to dry fresh herbs, whether they have originated from your garden or the store. In my practice, my most utilized method is air drying, but I will go over a few ideas you could try if you want to expedite the process. To air dry, you will need to store the herbs in an area in your home that has both warm and dry air. One method is to bundle the herbs and then hang them upside down until they become brittle. Another method is to separate the herbs and lay them on a rack to dry. This process takes approximately a week to complete, but more humid conditions could prolong the process.

Once the herbs are dry, you can crush them and store them in jars for later use. Pro tip: remember to label them. While I am able to identify my herbs by smell, this is a particular talent that took several years to master. To save yourself the hassle of not knowing which pile of dried green leaves are what, make sure to label them ahead of time.

If you happen to have a dehydrator, drying herbs is an excellent use for it. The herbs can be arranged on the layers of the dehydrator at the lowest setting available for approximately two to four hours. Some herbs hold more moisture and may have to be dried for longer than others. If you do not have a dehydrator, an oven will suffice! Arrange the herbs on a baking sheet in a single layer and put your oven on the lowest setting for approximately a half hour. Check on your herbs periodically. When they are completely dry, they will crumble to the touch.

HERB CORRESPONDENCES

Now that we have gone over how to grow, dry, or purchase our own herbs, it is time to delve into some of the common correspondences for herbs. In this section, I will include those already mentioned as well as the many herbs that popular brands do not have on standby. While store-bought herbs are a great starting point, sometimes you need to expand the contents of your at-home apothecary. These herbs can be used in tinctures, spell jars, kitchen witchery, dressing candles, and more. There is a vast array of possibilities when using herbs. While you may choose to forgo working with herbs altogether, this list is included to help you decide if you would like to and what you might like to have on hand for your workings.

Allspice: Luck, money, and prosperity

Basil: Love, peace, prosperity, and protection

Bay leaves: Divination, messengers, protection, and strength

Blue lotus: Higher consciousness, opening doors, peace, and protection

Calendula: Dream work, justice, protection, and psychic enhancement

Caraway: Fidelity, health, passion, and protection

Catnip: Beauty, happiness, love, and prophetic dreams

Cayenne: Baneful magick, fidelity, hex-breaking, and love

Celery: Psychic enhancement, sexuality, and strength

Chili powder: Baneful magick, fidelity, hex-breaking, and love

Chives: Banishing, health, and protection

Chamomile: Calm, peace, prosperity, and sleep

Cilantro: Healing, health, and love

Cinnamon: Love, manifestations, sexuality, speed, and success

Cloves: Banishing, love, money, and protection

Cumin: Anti-theft, fidelity, and protection

Curry: Energy, passion, and protection

Dandelions: Divination, love, and wishes

Dill: Good fortune, love, money, and protection

Dragon's blood: Love, increasing power, love, and protection

Fennel: Healing, protection, and purification

Frankincense: Protection, repelling negativity, and spirituality

Ginger: Prosperity, sexuality, and success

Juniper: Healing, love, and protection

Lavender: Happiness, protection, purification, and sleep

Marjoram: Happiness, health, money, and protection

Myrrh: Healing, protection, and spirituality

Mugwort: Dream work, healing, protection, psychic enhancement, and strength

Mustard: Courage, fertility, protection, and strength

Nutmeg: Health, luck, money, and psychic enhancement

Onion: Banishing, health, prophetic dreams, and protection

Oregano: Creativity, healing, love, and protection

Paprika: Energy and increasing power

Parsley: Inspiration, peace, protection, strength, and wealth

Pepper: Baneful magick, banishing, and protection

Poppy: Invisibility, luck, prosperity, and restful sleep

Rose: Beauty, healing, love, and protection

Rosemary: Banishing, mental clarity, protection, and purification

Sage: Healing, protection, purification, and wisdom

Salt: Protection and purification

Sesame: Good fortune, prosperity, and sexuality

Star anise: Luck and psychic enhancement

Tarragon: Compassion, love, and protection

Thyme: Courage, healing, psychic enhancement, and restful sleep

Turmeric: Banishing, protection, strength, and vitality

Valerian: Banishing, purification, repelling negative energy, and restful sleep

Vervain: Healing, love, peace, and prosperity

Yarrow: Courage, divination, love, and psychic enhancement

Yerba santa: Beauty, healing, protection, and psychic enhancement

essential oils

Another way of incorporating herbs into your practice is through the use of oils. Oils and essential oils are an excellent addition to spellwork. It needs to be noted that these oils are highly concentrated and can be irritating if they are applied directly to skin. When it comes to topical applications, you will need a carrier oil to dilute the formula. When you are applying oils directly to candles, use your judgment as to whether or not you should dilute them, but regardless, oils should be used sparingly. Some essential oils are highly flammable, and you must stay with your candles for the duration of the spells if you are attached to your home not being engulfed in flames. Remember, safety first!

Basil: Grief, happiness, peace, and prosperity

Bergamot: Balancing emotions, calming, money, and protection

Cardamom: Alleviating mental fatigue, energy, love, sexuality, and uplifting

Cedarwood: Balancing emotions, calming anger, and enhancing spirituality

Chamomile: Healing, meditation, peace, prosperity, and success

Cinnamon: Alleviating depression and fatigue, blessings, money, and psychic awareness

Clary sage: Balance, dream work, and happiness

Clove: Courage, emotional support, protection, and well-being

Coriander: Anti-anxiety, fidelity, healing, happiness, and love

Cypress: Blessings, healing, mental clarity, and protection

Eucalyptus: Grief, healing, purification, and well-being

Frankincense: Banishing negativity, focusing energy, justice, and spiritual growth

Geranium: Emotional support, happiness, peace, and protection

Ginger: Courage, grounding, mental fatigue, prosperity, and sexuality

Grapefruit: Happiness, emotional balance, happiness, purification, and well-being

Jasmine: Love, peace, psychic awareness, sexuality, and spirituality

Juniper: Healing, protection, and purification

Lavender: Balancing emotions, healing, love, and peace

Lemon: Energy, happiness, prosperity, and success

Lemongrass: Grounding, luck, psychic awareness, and purification

Lime: Energizing, protection, purification, and uplifting

Myrrh: Abundance, grief, healing, meditation, peace, spirituality, and success

Orange: Clarity, energy, happiness, purification, solar energy, and vitality

Patchouli: Justice, love, money, repelling negative energy, and sexuality

Peppermint: Banishing negativity, healing, justice, prosperity, purification, and uplifting

Pine: Abundance, healing, protection, and purification

Rose: Attracting love, beauty, desire, peace, and sexuality

Rosemary: Banishing negativity, grief, healing, intuition, love, and mental clarity

Sandalwood: Banishing negativity, grief, healing, justice, peace, sexuality, and well-being

Tea tree: Banishing negativity, emotional balance, healing, and mental clarity

Thyme: Grief, grounding, happiness, love, luck, and uplifting

Vetiver: Grounding, prosperity, releasing toxic emotions, stability, and tranquility

Ylang-ylang: Adjusting to change, happiness, love, peace, sexuality, and soothing anger

Baneful Herbs

Baneful herbs, as the name implies, are herbs that can be harmful—if not fatal—because they are poisonous. Baneful herbs are often used in ointments for their hallucinogenic properties. These salves or balms are commonly referred to as "flying ointments." However, baneful herbs are also widely used in banishing and cursing.

I have no qualms with hexing or cursing, provided the intended target is deserving and there is a rigorous review of the validity. If you put forth the energy to assert just cause, I must assume you have done your homework. Equally, whether or not you work baneful magic is none of my business. I am also a firm believer in balance—day and night, light and darkness, above and below—so I could not exclude these beautiful baneful counterparts. If my own home was not littered with pets and human goblins, I would most certainly have my own baneful garden for the herbs' sheer majesty.

However, due to the highly poisonous nature of these herbs, their use is not recommended unless you are willing to study further. Remember, there are reports of accidental deaths from the use of these plants, and they are not worth the risks unless you are astute in your working knowledge of how to care for and use them without unsubscribing from life. These plants are primarily known for their protective properties, but if you are unaware of how to handle them properly, they will do the opposite and harm.

Sound daunting? It is supposed to, so proceed with caution while I cover some baneful ground. Many of these herbs fall into the nightshade category. While the name itself can sound foreboding or mysterious, there are several plants in the nightshade family that you may consume on a regular basis. These include foods such as tomatoes, eggplants, peppers, and certain potatoes as well as tobacco.[39] While the term *nightshade* may conjure up a specific thought of poison, the term actually covers a variety of plants in the Solanaceae family that range from edible to deadly.

There is no family more prevalent in the dark history of witchcraft than that of the nightshade family. It is thought that the term *Solanaceae* originates from the Latin verb *solare*, which means *to soothe*, but these origins are unconfirmed.[40] This is a plant family that is steeped with mythological ties and has been linked to the garden of Hekate, Circe, and Medea.[41] In fact, it is thought that nightshades were of particular interest to Hekate, the Greek goddess of the night and witchcraft.

The following list is not exclusive to the nightshade family, so you will find other plant families as well, some of which are also thought to have ties to Hekate. Regardless of this connection, these plants have roots in both historical use as well as in mythology. I will cover these in an abbreviated detail while going over some of their magickal properties as well.

And, because it deserves repeating, do not handle these herbs without an in-depth knowledge of how to do so without poisoning yourself.

---

39. "The Powerful Solanaceae," United States Department of Agriculture.
40. Rehman, "Old.amu.ac.in."
41. Michael, *The Poison Path Herbal*, 3.

Belladonna

Belladonna, or *Atropa belladonna*, is a poisonous herb in the nightshade family. It has several folkloric names, some of which have an ominous tone, while others are deceiving. These names include banewort, fair lady, deadly nightshade, death's-herb, and devil's cherries.[42] This plant is thought to have both Saturn and Mars energy as a correspondence, which makes it a powerful plant ally if utilized with extreme caution. This plant has a history of being associated with witchcraft, death, and protection. And while this plant is one of protection, it was also used for spirit work and astral travel as this herb has hallucinogenic properties in small dosages.[43]

Uses: Astral projection, energy, expansion, and visions

Datura

Datura, or *Datura stramonium*, goes by many folk names as well. Some of the common folk names for this plant are devil's-apple, devil's-weed, ghost flower, Jimsonweed, sorcerer's herb, and *yerba del diablo*, which is Spanish for "herb of the devil." This plant is also in the nightshade family and is ruled by Saturn.[44] This herb was commonly used for breaking spells and warding against evil spirits, and its beautiful blooms are captivating to observe. This gives the plant the vibe of being a calculated enchantress. However, beauty should not always be equated with goodness, and that is the case with this plant as it is also quite lethal. Even so, datura has been used to induce trance states and visions for some, and thanks to its aura of enchantment, it has served the purpose of luring love and desire toward the spellcaster.[45]

Uses: Divination, enchantment, hex-breaking, and protection

Foxglove

Foxglove, or *Digitalis purpurea*, has several folk names, and the vast majority of them are related to the fae. Some of these alternative names include fairy fingers, fairy thimbles, and fairy weed as well as witch's bells, goblin's gloves, and

---

42. Cunningham, "Folk Names Cross-Reference," 289–307.
43. Wigington, "Magical Herbal Correspondences."
44. Cunningham, "Folk Names Cross-Reference," 289–307.
45. Ward, "Devil's Apple," *Poisoner's Apothecary.*

witches'-thimbles.[46] It is an herb rife with folkloric mysticism. The cups of the flowers were thought to house fairies within them, and this is frequently depicted in works of art.[47] Foxglove is ruled by Venus, and with this comes an element of love, giving it uses for matters of the heart. But, as it is poisonous, this herb is one of protection, whether it be the garden it is planted in or the home it is grown by.

Uses: Healing, love, and protection

Hellebore

Hellebore, or *Helleborus niger,* is a poisonous plant that also is referred to as Christmas rose, winter rose, and melampode. The name itself is a tribute to its poisonous nature as it is a combination of *helien,* which means "to kill," and *bora,* meaning "food."[48] As is common with baneful herbs, its primary use was that of protection and warding off evil spirits, and it was even thought to render the user invisible. This plant has a strong bond to the spirit world, and it was even thought to have medicinal purposes in ancient Greece. There it was considered an anecdote to mania and demonic possession.[49] This plant is one of the few in this section that is not in the nightshade family. Hellebore is, instead, a part of the *Ranunculaceae* family or, in layman's terms, the buttercup family.[50] Fortunately the foul taste of these plants is a strong deterrent to accidentally overdosing on them.

Uses: Astral projection, invisibility, and protection

Henbane

Henbane, or *Hyoscyamus niger,* has several alternative names, such as devil's eye, henbells, Jupiter's bean, and black nightshade.[51] As the last folk name suggests, this plant belongs to the nightshade family. This herb has hallucinogenic properties and was used for astral travel, sleep, and pain relief. In Greek mythology, those who wandered the river Styx were crowned with henbane to make them

---

46. Cunningham, "Folk Names Cross-Reference," 289–307.
47. Inkwright, *Botanical Curses and Poisons,* 240.
48. Ward, "The Court of Helleborus," *Poisoner's Apothecary.*
49. Ward, "The Court of Helleborus," *Poisoner's Apothecary.*
50. The Editors of *Encyclopaedia Britannica,* "Hellebore."
51. Cunningham, "Folk Names Cross-Reference," 289–307.

forget their previous lives.[52] This was due to its actual association with inducing forgetfulness in real life. As a baneful herb, henbane was also used in protection magick as well as in bindings and spirit work.

Uses: Binding, love, protection, and spirit work

Mandrake

Mandrake, or *Atropa mandragora*, had many folk names as well. Some of these names included alraun, brain thief, womandrake, sorcerer's root, and herb of Circe.[53] It is easy to see that this herb has mythological ties with its moniker of *herb of Circe*, and it has ties to not only Circe but Hekate and Medea as well. In some traditions, the name *alraun* was given to plants with root systems that resembled humans, much like those of mandrake. The title *alraun* also has a connection with runes and witchcraft in general.[54]

Historical references to this plant are plentiful, and this plant is even mentioned in the book of Genesis in the Old Testament, but it is also mentioned in contemporary literature such as the *Harry Potter* series.[52] This plant also had many medicinal uses due to its anesthetic properties, though the applications were not inherently humane. Many times, this anesthetic was used to prolong the death process to ensure maximum suffering. As with the other herbs included in this section, mandrake was also known for its hallucinogenic properties, which made it useful for inducing trancelike states and altering consciousness to induce visions.

Uses: Health, prosperity, and protection

Wolfsbane

Wolfsbane, or *Aconitum napellus*, *Aconitum columbianum*, or *Aconitum lamarckii*, *among others*, had many fun folkloric names, such as aconite, cupid's car, Dumbledore's delight, and Thor's hat, but do not let this be a distraction from the fact the herb is, indeed, poisonous.[55] This plant is in the *Ranunculaceae* family and is another on this list that is not in the nightshade family. This plant is useful in spiritual work and has healing properties despite its baneful applications. As with

---

52. Inkwright, *Botanical Curses and Poisons*, 149.
53. Cunningham, "Folk Names Cross-Reference," 289–307.
54. Ward, "A Collection of Mandrake Folklore," *Poisoner's Apothecary*.
55. Cunningham, "Folk Names Cross-Reference," 289–307.

the other baneful plants, there is a rich mythological history with this plant as well. One myth tells of when Athena sprinkled *aconite* on the maiden Arachne, transforming her into a spider.[56] This story is meant to portray the transformative properties of this herb, which is used to shapeshift in some traditions. Wolfsbane is also another of the herbs considered sacred to Hekate, Circe, and Medea. This herb is also called the "Queen of Poisons" as it is a potent poison, capable of killing a person quickly.[57] This herb, as well as the others comprising this list, is also considered a plant of protection. It is often used as such and is even thought to render the user invisible.

Uses: Healing, protection, and spirit work

HERBAL CODE NAMES

This section is included for the pure enjoyment of the alternate names for plants. You have likely heard the phrases "eye of newt or "toe of frog" before, be it in a Shakespearean production or movies and novels pertaining to witches. If you have ever scratched your head at what those plants may be, this section is for you. These terms are not literal, but rather, they are code names for flowers and herbs. Many of the terms, such as *toe* or *tongue*, refer to the specific part of the plant that is needed, such as a leaf or petal.

This list can be a way to add historical traditionalism to your workings, or it can just be a list to explore so you can drop the terms into the conversation and confuse the other participant. No matter what you are hoping to achieve, it is undoubtedly interesting to dig into the past names for some of the herbs that we are familiar with today.

This list is largely an abridged version of the Folk Names Cross-Reference section found in Scott Cunningham's *Encyclopedia of Magical Herbs.*[58]

Absinthe: Wormwood

Ass's ear: Comfrey

Ass's foot: Coltsfoot

Bat's wing: Holly leaves

---

56. Inkwright, *Botanical Curses and Poisons*, 242.
57. Inkwright, *Botanical Curses and Poisons*, 240.
58. Cunningham, "Folk Names Cross-Reference," 289–307.

Bear's foot: Lady's mantle

Bee balm: Lemon balm

Beer flower: Hops

Bindweed: Morning glory

Bird's-eye: Pansy

Bird's-foot: Fenugreek

Bird's nest: Carrot

Blindeyes: Poppy

Blind worm's sting: Knotweed

Bloody fingers: Foxglove

Bride of the sun: Calendula

Calf's snout: Snapdragon

Cat's-foot: Ground ivy

Cat's wort: Catnip

Crow's foot: Wild geranium

Devil plant: Basil

Devil's dung: Asafoetida

Devil's eye: Henbane

Devil's nettle: Yarrow

Dew of the sea: Rosemary

Drunkard: Marigold

Elf leaf: Lavender

Englishman's foot: Common plantain

Eye of newt: Mustard seed

Fair lady: Belladonna

Fairy finger: Foxglove

Graveyard dust: Mullein

Graveyard flowers: Plumeria

Ground apple: Chamomile

Hag's taper: Mullein

Herb of Circe: Mandrake

Herb of enchantment: Vervain

Juno's tears: Vervain

Lady of the woods: Birch

Lady's key: Cowslip

Lady's mantle: Yarrow

Lion's foot: Lady's mantle

Lion's-mouth: Foxglove

Lion's-tooth: Dandelion

Mother of the herbs: Rue

Naughty man: Mugwort

Naughty man's cherries: Belladonna

Nosebleed: Yarrow

Old-man's-flannel: Mullein

Old-man's-pepper: Yarrow

Old uncle Henry: Mugwort

Raccoonberry: Mandrake

Serpent's-tongue: Adder's-tongue

Sparrow's tongue: Knotweed

Tongue of dog: Hounds tongue

Witches' aspirin: White willow bark

Witches' bells: Foxglove

Witches' berry: Belladonna

Witches' broom: Mistletoes

Witches' herb: Basil

Witches' thimble: Datura

Witch herb: Mugwort

Witchwood: Rowan

Broom Closet Witch Tips

. . . .

If you thought crystals were easy to conceal, herbs are even easier, and they open the gateway to a vast array of witchy practices, such as kitchen witchery, spellwork, and ritual baths. Gardening is not an innately witchy practice, but the act of tending to a garden can be highly spiritual as it allows a direct connection with the earth as well as the individual energies of the plants you choose to grow. Furthermore, keeping a small herb garden indoors is also a great way to connect to the herbs themselves for those who live in cities!

The herbs you grow can then be made useful in simple kitchen witchery, which consists of intentionally crafting your meals and teas with specific intentions. Kitchen witchery is an easily concealed practice as we all must eat to sustain life. By making use of kitchen magick, we can create an altar in our kitchens. Herbs and salt represent the earth, pots or cups stand for water, and, depending on your tradition, wooden spoons and knives can represent either fire or air. It's quite simple to pair this daily need to eat with our practice, letting us go undetected if we're not ready for our identities to be revealed.

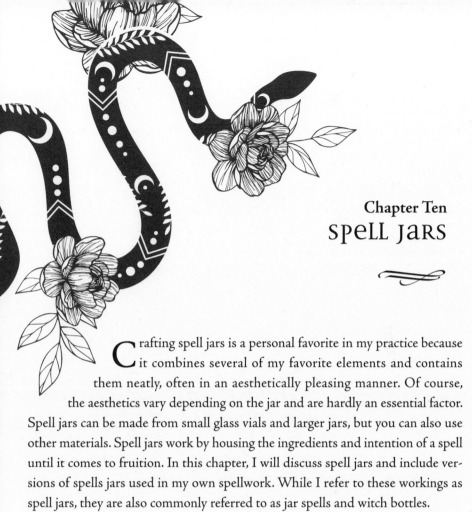

spell jars

Crafting spell jars is a personal favorite in my practice because it combines several of my favorite elements and contains them neatly, often in an aesthetically pleasing manner. Of course, the aesthetics vary depending on the jar and are hardly an essential factor. Spell jars can be made from small glass vials and larger jars, but you can also use other materials. Spell jars work by housing the ingredients and intention of a spell until it comes to fruition. In this chapter, I will discuss spell jars and include versions of spells jars used in my own spellwork. While I refer to these workings as spell jars, they are also commonly referred to as jar spells and witch bottles.

HISTORY

Witch bottles are thought to date back to approximately the seventeenth century and were made of stoneware or glass.[59] Historically these bottles were meant for protection, and as such, they would include protective materials, such as shards of glass, nails, and needles. These jars also included contents from either the individuals they were protecting or the individuals believed to have cast the evil. These personal effects were often hair, urine, teeth, or nail clippings.[60] These protective bottles would either be buried near the doorstep or placed by the hearth to protect the home from evil. The bottles placed by the hearth would heat up, and

---

59. "'Witch Bottles' Concealed and Revealed."
60. "'Witch Bottles' Concealed and Revealed."

heating them was thought to send the negative energy straight back to whoever had cast it in the first place.[61]

The fact that many witch bottles date back to the 1600s in England means they were likely made in the midst of the witch panic era.[62] Due to the beliefs of the time, most unfavorable external happenings were attributed to witchcraft and the paranormal, and it makes sense that many of the original witch bottles were thought to have been for both protection and healing. It is also thought that many of these bottles were made by nonpractitioners, and their original purpose, instead, was to deter witches from entering their homes either literally or through the astral. These bottles were also thought of as protection from curses or hexes being cast against them. It's also worth noting that archaeological discoveries of witch bottles are not exclusive to England, and there have been some unearthed in North America as well.[63]

creatinç spell jars

In modern times, witch bottles and spell jars have become a mainstay in many traditions, and they have become a reworking of past eras as the witch is now making the bottles for themselves rather than for protection against outside forces. These modern bottles are extremely versatile as they can serve a variety of functions and can be made with nearly any sized vessel you would prefer. This means spell jars can even be portable for spells you would like to keep on you, be they spells for protection, self-love, or anything in between. The vessel itself serves to keep the contents of the spell confined, letting them interact and build upon each other until the spell materializes. In honoring the workings of the past, these modern spell jars can also be used to contain negative energy or to send any negative energy back.

When it comes to the containers, you can be as resourceful or as extravagant as you like. Just keep in mind the type of spell that you are working and what containers might be appropriate. For example, a medicine bottle makes a useful apparatus for spells involving health and healing, whereas if the spells are for love and

61. Berard, "Civil War-Era Bottle Found on Highway Median May Be Rare 'Witch Bottle.'"
62. Daley, "'Witch Bottle' Filled with Teeth, Pins and Mysterious Liquid Discovered in English Chimeny."
63. Becker, "An American Witch Bottle."

attraction, you might repurpose a perfume bottle. Remember, symbolism is an important aspect to spellwork as items themselves have correspondences. While there is a variety of resources you can use for determining the correspondences for planets, signs, elements, herbs, and crystals, there is also a wealth of personal symbolism to tap into within your own practice.

spell jar placement

One of the questions that I come across most frequently goes something like this: "Okay, I've made the spell jar. Now what?" As with most spellwork, this question depends on what the intention of the spell is. Having a clear intention will assist you in knowing exactly what you need to do with the jar once it has been created. Certain spells will do best nearby, while others will benefit from being sent away.

Some common placements nearby would be on a nightstand, on an altar, or in some other location within your home. Some spell jars benefit from being on your person in the form of jewelry, being carried in your bag, or being with you in your car. Others may do best if they are sent away from you, either left or buried at a location.

For spell jars that involve home protection or bringing in good fortune to your abode, you may choose to bury the jar to disperse the energy. If this is the method you choose, you do not want to bury items such as glass, salt, or anything else that could be potentially harmful to the environment. After all, modern glass takes approximately four thousand years to deteriorate.[64] Always exercise caution when choosing the container. Some suitable replacements for glass jars include hollowed-out eggshells or fruits as well as biodegradable tea cloth or even some paper materials.

If you have made a spell jar for lucid dreaming or to rid yourself of nightmares, the best placement for it would be close to where you sleep, such as on your nightstand or under your pillow. If you have made a spell for self-love, this jar would benefit from being made into jewelry or carried in your bag so that you can always have it with you. This approach would also do well with safe travel spell jars.

Perhaps you are performing glamour magick, or your jar serves a beauty function. In this case, place your jar in your bathroom, on your vanity, or wherever it is that you spend your time getting ready for the day. Maybe you have cast a

---

64. Cole, "Is Glass Biodegradable & Is It Better than Plastic?"

spell to attract positivity to your home or to affect your relationship with those in your home, be it your spouse, roommates, children, or whomever. You can place these jars in the rooms where you spend most of your time together, whichever rooms those may be.

When your spells have come to fruition or served their purposes, you can dispose of them mindfully. When deconstructing my jars, I cleanse the jars and any crystals in them for later use. I then dispose of any salt in the garbage and burn any herbs or return them to the earth. My disposal methods may vary with the purpose of the jar, and I do repurpose what I can each time. In my own practice, crystals and jars can be repurposed for several spells. The only exception I might make is in the case of a Return to Sender Jar, and that is purely to assure that the energy is permanently cleared from my space. While I *could* cleanse the materials, this is a matter of preference and beliefs.

the spells

In this section, I will share my favorite spell jars. In each spell, I will use measurements of a "pinch," and I will often encourage you to choose a jar that works for you. Based on the size of the jar, you can then use as little or as much of the ingredients listed to create a jar that you are proud of. While I will list these steps individually under almost every spell jar, you must first choose your jar, which won't be included in the materials list. After choosing your jar, you will need to cleanse your jar. One popular method for cleansing smaller jars is to make use of incense and use the smoke to clear the stagnant energy. If you would like to use an alternative method, chapter 8 lists several methods that you can choose from. As you're encouraged to use whichever method for cleansing that you prefer, those materials won't be included in the material lists either.

Witchcraft in Action
self-love spell jar

This Self-Love Spell Jar is to be used when you need to attract a little more love and kindness in your own direction. After all, loving ourselves is the first step in being able to give love properly and receive love properly. I recommend doing this spell jar alongside some shadow work, which you can learn more about in chapter 14, and placing this jar on your nightstand, putting in your purse or bag, or making jewelry out of it so you can always keep the jar with you.

Materials:

* Pinch of pink Himalayan salt (to foster love)
* Pinch of dried rose petals (for self-love and attracting good fortune)
* Pinch of dried lavender (for reducing anxiety and increasing awareness)
* Pinch of dried rosemary (for strength)
* Pinch of rose quartz chips or pieces (for love)
* Pink candle (optional)
* Lighter or matches (optional)

Directions:

1. As always, the first step is choosing a jar or container that suits your needs. Most often, I use small 10-milliliter jars to help me conserve ingredients.
2. Cleanse your jar using your preferred method. One common method is using incense or herb bundles and filling the jar with the smoke.
3. Start adding the ingredients, beginning with the Himalayan salt. Salt can be damaging to crystals, so I use this as my first layer. Give the salt its intention while you're adding it by stating that the Himalayan salt is for fostering love.
4. Add the rose petals and recite that they are to foster self-love and attract good fortune.
5. Add the lavender and state that it is to reduce anxiety, increase your awareness, and usher in a feeling of calm.
6. Add the rosemary and recite that it is for strength and clarity.
7. Add the rose quartz chips or pieces and state that they're for love for yourself and humanity.
8. If you would like, you can seal this jar with pink candle wax for love and affection.

Witchcraft in Action
PROTECTION SPELL JAR

You should always carry protection, and by this I mean spell jars, protective crystals, banishing sprays, amulets, or whatever it is that makes you feel safe and creates a barrier. There are some foul energies out there, whether they be spiritual or otherwise, and having protections in place is a necessary part of your practice when delving into magick—as well as just simply existing. In short, protecting ourselves and our energies is necessary. I have several versions of this jar, and I place them on my person, in my vehicle, and around my home strategically to keep my barriers in place.

Materials:
* Pinch of black salt (to dispel negative energy)
* Pinch of dried basil (for protection, fostering loving vibrations, and warding off negativity)
* 1 or 2 dried bay leaves (for protection, healing, and strength)
* Pinch of dried garden sage (for cleansing, protection, and blessings)
* Pinch of amethyst crystal chips or pieces (for protection, healing, and purification)
* Pinch of obsidian crystal chips or pieces (for protection and warding off negativity)
* Black candle (optional)
* Lighter or matches (optional)

Directions:
1. Choose your jar or container.
2. Cleanse your jar with your preferred method.
3. Add the black salt to the jar and give it its purpose by saying that it is to dispel negative energy.
4. Add the basil and state that it is to foster loving vibrations, offer protection, and to ward off negativity.

5. Add one or two bay leaves and give the ingredient its purpose by stating that it is for protection, healing, and strength.

6. Add the garden sage and state that it is for cleansing, protection, and blessings.

7. Add the amethyst crystal chips or pieces and tell them that they are for protection, healing, and purification.

8. Add the obsidian crystal chips or pieces and recite that they are for protection and warding off negativity.

9. If you would like, you can seal this jar with black candle wax for protection.

Witchcraft in Action
PROSPERITY SPELL JAR

Could you use a little more prosperity in your life? It seems most of us, excluding the 1 percent, could benefit from a cosmic boost straight into our pockets from time to time. The following is a jar to be used to bring prosperity to you. While I've not hit it big playing the lottery (*and I do hear that you have to actually play the lottery to win*) I make use of this spell jar when I need a little extra to cushion my pockets, be it for an expense I wasn't prepared for or for those combat boots I've had my eye on. This is a spell to reduce restraints toward money and to get money flowing in your direction. I recommend keeping this jar near your wallet or purse to draw money your way. Alternatively, if the jar itself is too clunky, you could use a sachet in the same way.

Materials:
* Pinch of sea salt (for purification)
* Pinch of dried thyme (to attract wealth)
* Pinch of dried mint (for attracting business, prosperity, and success)
* Pinch of ground cinnamon (for drawing money quickly)
* Pinch of citrine chips or pieces (for wealth and abundance)

* Pinch of green aventurine chips or pieces (for prosperous energy)
* At least 1 or 2 coins (to attract more wealth)
* Green candle (optional)
* Lighter or matches (optional)

Directions:

1. The first step is choosing your jar or container. For this spell, you will need a jar with a wide enough opening to fit the coins.
2. Cleanse your jar with your preferred method.
3. Add the sea salt and recite that it is for purification.
4. Add the thyme and recite that it is for attracting wealth into your life.
5. Add the mint and recite that it is for attracting business, prosperity, and success into your life.
6. Add the ground cinnamon and recite that it is for drawing money quickly.
7. Add the citrine chips or pieces and recite that they are for wealth and abundance.
8. Add the green aventurine chips or pieces and recite that they are for prosperous energy.
9. Add one or two coins, or however many will fit, and state that this ingredient is to attract more wealth.
10. If you would like, you can light the green candle and seal the jar with its wax for prosperity.

Witchcraft in Action
creativity spell jar

If you are experiencing a creativity block or would simply like to attract a higher flow state and tap into your inner creativity, this is the spell jar for you. As humans, we have an innate desire to create. Now, what we decide to create varies from individual to individual, but the desire is consistent. However, sometimes we have a blockage that prevents us from achieving that creative flow we breathe for. Think of it as "writer's block" but applicable to more than just writing. This spell aims to correct this block and open the pathways to enhance our creativity and allow it to flow more easily to us.

Materials:
* Pinch of Himalayan salt (for positive energy)
* Pinch of dried rosemary (for creativity boost)
* Pinch of dried rose petals (for self-confidence and creativity)
* Pinch of dried cloves (to clear the mind and creative blocks)
* Pinch of citrine chips or pieces (for motivation and creativity)
* Pinch of carnelian chips or pieces (for energy flow and vitality)
* Pinch of sodalite chips or pieces (for self-expression)
* Orange candle (optional)
* Lighter or matches (optional)

Directions:
1. Choose your jar or container.
2. Cleanse your jar using your preferred method.
3. Add the Himalayan salt and recite that it is for promoting positive energy.
4. Add the rosemary and recite that it is for boosting creativity.
5. Add the rose petals and recite that they are for self-confidence and enhancing creativity.
6. Add the cloves and recite that they are to clear the mind and any creative blocks.
7. Add the citrine chips or pieces and recite that they are for enhancing motivation and encouraging creativity.
8. Add the carnelian chips or pieces and recite that they are for allowing the energy to flow and for enhancing vitality.
9. Add the sodalite chips or pieces and state that are to enhance self-expression.
10. If you would like, you can seal this jar with orange candle wax for creativity.

Witchcraft in Action
safe travel spell jar

Got upcoming travel plans? Create this spell jar to ensure not only safe travels but happy travels as well. I do not know about your family, but I know traveling has always made my own family tense—both as a child passenger and the adult driver. Furthermore, I once served a summer working in hospitality. The last adjective I would use to describe people on vacation is *hospitable*. I have several other choice words for them, but I digress. Maybe you are traveling for reasons other than vacation, and that's just as well. This spell jar's mission is to solve two problems simultaneously regardless.

Materials:
* Pinch of sea salt (for purification and positive energy)
* Pinch of dried lavender (for promoting harmony and reducing anxiety)
* Pinch of dried mint (for a successful trip)
* Pinch of dried orange peel (for happiness)
* Pinch of dried garden sage (to repel negative energy)
* Pinch of dried, ground eggshells (for protection)
* Pinch of tiger's-eye chips or pieces (for protection)
* Black candle (optional)
* Lighter or matches (optional)

Directions:
1. As always, the first step is to choose your jar or container.
2. Cleanse your jar using your preferred method.
3. Add the sea salt and recite that it is for purification and promoting positive energy.
4. Add the lavender and recite that it is for reducing anxiety and promoting harmony.
5. Add the mint and recite that it is for a successful journey.
6. Add the orange peel and recite that it is to encourage happiness.

7. Add the garden sage and recite that it is to repel negative energy.

8. Add the eggshells and recite that they are for protection on your journey.

9. Add the tiger's-eye chips or pieces and recite that they are for protection.

10. If you would like, you can seal this spell jar with black candle wax for protection.

Witchcraft in Action
PSYCHIC SPELL JAR

Wanting to tap into your third eye? This spell is crafted to assist you in doing just that. This spell is used to enhance your third eye as well as to move blockages that inhibit you from accessing this information more easily. To use this spell jar once it is created, you could meditate while holding it or place it nearby. Alternatively, if prophetic dreams are what you are seeking, place this spell jar near where you sleep—either on a nightstand, under your pillow, or under your bed. You get the idea.

Materials:
* Pinch of black salt (for psychic protection)
* Pinch of dried thyme (to attract psychic abilities and increase your intuition)
* Pinch of dried mugwort (to enhance psychic powers and for protection)
* 1 or 2 star anise pods (for spiritual connection and psychic abilities)
* Pinch of moonstone crystal chips or pieces (for clairvoyance and intuition)
* Pinch of amethyst crystal chips or pieces (for channeling and heightening psychic powers)

* Pinch of fluorite crystal chips or pieces (for unblocking energy and to act as a psychic shield)
* Purple candle (optional)
* Lighter or matches (optional)

Directions:

1. Choose your jar or container.
2. Cleanse your jar using your preferred method.
3. Add the black salt and recite that it is for psychic protection.
4. Add the thyme and recite that it is to attract psychic abilities and increase your intuition.
5. Add the mugwort and recite that it is to enhance psychic powers and for protection.
6. Add one or two star anise pods and recite that the ingredient is for enhancing your spiritual connection and increasing your psychic abilities.
7. Add the moonstone crystal chips or pieces and recite that they are for clairvoyance and strengthening your intuition.
8. Add the amethyst chips or pieces and recite that they are for channeling and heightening your psychic powers.
9. Add the fluorite chips or pieces and recite that they are to unblock energy and act as a psychic shield.
10. If you would like, you can seal this jar with purple candle wax for intuition and wisdom.

Witchcraft in Action
HEALING SPELL JAR

This spell jar can be used as a preventive measure, but it can also be used once an illness or incident has occurred to lessen the overall effects. The purpose of this jar is to help foster healing energy. This can be necessary for various reasons and ailments, such as an illness or trauma. Empty medicine jars or bottles can make great canisters for containing this spell, but you can use whatever you have at your disposal.

Materials:
* Pinch of sea salt (for cleansing and protection)
* Pinch of dried chamomile (to promote healing and increase health)
* Pinch of dried calendula (for immunity and defense)
* Pinch of dried cloves (to attract good health)
* Pinch of citrine chips or pieces (for revitalization and absorbing negative energy)
* Pinch of clear quartz chips or pieces (for balance)
* Green candle (optional)
* Lighter or matches (optional)

Directions:
1. Choose your jar or container.
2. Cleanse your jar using your preferred method.
3. Add the sea salt and recite that it is for cleansing and protection.
4. Add the chamomile and recite that it is to promote healing and increase health.
5. Add the calendula and recite that it is for boosting immunity and defense.
6. Add the cloves and recite that they are to attract good health—mental and physical.
7. Add the citrine crystal chips or pieces and recite that they are for revitalization and absorbing negativity.
8. Add the clear quartz crystal chips or pieces and recite that they are to restore balance in the body and mind.
9. If you would like, you can seal this jar with green candle wax for healing.

Witchcraft in Action
success spell jar

Need a little more success in your life? Here is a spell jar for just that. What success means varies from person to person, so make sure to be specific in your intentions when creating this jar. The universe has been known to answer vague requests in interesting ways. If you have a specific outcome in mind, be sure to clarify what it is that you are seeking by understanding exactly what success means to you and what success looks like for you. Be clear about what you are after so it is easier to manifest just that.

Materials:
* Pinch of sea salt (for cleansing and protection)
* Pinch of dried chamomile (for promoting growth, attracting success, and enhancing self-confidence)
* Pinch of dried mint (for attracting money and mental clarity)
* Pinch of dried basil (for strength and luck)
* Pinch of dried cloves (for success)
* Pinch of citrine crystal chips or pieces (for abundance)
* Pinch of labradorite chips or pieces (for strength and perseverance)
* Red candle (optional)
* Lighter or matches (optional)

Directions:
1. Choose your jar or container.
2. Cleanse your jar using your preferred method.
3. Add the sea salt and recite that it is for cleansing and protection.
4. Add the chamomile and recite that it is to promote growth, attract success, and enhance self-confidence.
5. Add the mint and recite that it is for attracting money and achieving mental clarity.

6. Add the basil and recite that it is to increase strength and attract good fortune.

7. Add the cloves and recite that they are to bring forth success.

8. Add the citrine crystal chips or pieces and recite that they are for attracting abundance.

9. Add the labradorite crystal chips or pieces and recite that they are for encouraging strength and perseverance.

10. If you would like, you can seal this jar with red candle wax for action and willpower.

Witchcraft in Action
sweet dreams spell jar

A restful night's sleep is necessary. And sweet dreams? Even better. I have personally struggled with insomnia for the better portion of my life as well as some intense nightmares. If I am in a particular bout of repetitious nightmares, I'll craft the following spell jar to help alleviate some of the stressors in my subconscious mind. I recommend pairing this spell with dream journaling to dissect the themes of your dreams for symbolism and to uncover hidden meanings. Place this spell jar on your nightstand, underneath your pillow, or below your bed for maximum effect.

Materials:
* Pinch of sea salt (for cleansing and protection)
* Pinch of dried lavender (for restful sleep and healing)
* Pinch of dried chamomile (for relaxation and calming energy)
* Pinch of dried garden sage (for protection and blessing)
* Pinch of amethyst crystal chips or pieces (for serene energy)
* Pinch of selenite crystal chips or pieces (to combat insomnia)
* Blue candle (optional)
* Lighter or matches (optional)

Directions:

1. Choose your jar or container.
2. Cleanse your jar using your preferred method.
3. Add the sea salt and recite that it is for cleansing and protection.
4. Add the lavender and recite that it is for restful sleep and healing.
5. Add the chamomile and recite that it is to induce relaxation and produce calming energy.
6. Add the garden sage and recite that it is for protection and blessings.
7. Add the amethyst crystal chips or pieces and recite that they are to create an energy of serenity.
8. Add the selenite crystal chips or pieces and recite that they are to combat insomnia and to get a good night's sleep.
9. If you would like, you can seal this jar with blue candle wax for peace.

Witchcraft in Action
mood boost spell jar

At times, the air and energy around us are stagnant, and they create negative spaces for us to dwell in both physically and within our psyche. This spell is a good way to shift the energy around you in a positive way. I use this jar when I have been in a self-described "funk," and I just need a pick-me-up to get me by.

This jar is not a suitable replacement for proper mental health care, and I advocate for both professional care and spellwork when tackling issues such as mental health or shadow work.

Materials:

* Pinch of black salt (to banish negativity)
* Pinch of dried holy basil (for uplifting spirits and positive energy)

* Pinch of dried lemon balm (for happiness)
* Pinch of dried lavender (for peace and decreasing anxiety)
* Pinch of dried roses (for self-love and compassion)
* Pinch of citrine crystal chips or pieces (for energy and vitality)
* Pinch of carnelian crystal chips or pieces (for invigoration and happiness)
* Orange or yellow candle (optional)
* Lighter or matches (optional)

Directions:

1. Choose your jar or container.
2. Cleanse your jar using your preferred method.
3. Add the black salt and recite that it is to banish negativity.
4. Add the holy basil and recite that it is to uplift your spirits and increase positive energy.
5. Add the lemon balm and recite that it is to promote happiness.
6. Add the lavender and recite that it is for fostering peace and decreasing anxiety.
7. Add the roses and recite that they are for attracting self-love and compassion.
8. Add the citrine crystal chips or pieces and recite that they are for increasing energy and vitality.
9. Add the carnelian crystal chips or pieces and recite that they are for invigoration and happiness.
10. If you would like, you can seal this spell jar with orange or yellow candle wax for happiness.

Broom Closet Witch Tips

Admittedly, hiding spell jars can be difficult. However, while that is true, it is not impossible. If you need to hide your spell jars, it might be best to focus on using biodegradable materials for your containers, such as eggshells, fruits, or even cardboard toilet paper rolls. When using biodegradable containers and fillings, you can discretely bury your spellwork to disperse its energy. If this is the option you choose, remember to be mindful not to use salt as it can be harmful to the soil.

If you enjoy the look of spell bottles, you can attempt to pass them off as home decor. It is true, spell jars are often beautiful, and jar decor is not exactly uncommon. Sand art jars, which were crafted from layers of colored sand, were everywhere in the '90s, and there seems to be no shortage of mason jar obsessions in modern times. You may even be able to portray these items as being in the same vein as a terrarium if pressed.

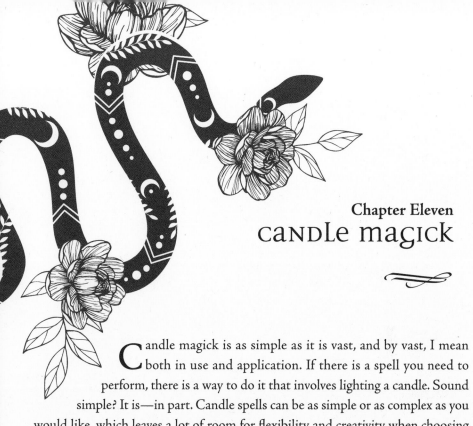

candle magick

Candle magick is as simple as it is vast, and by vast, I mean both in use and application. If there is a spell you need to perform, there is a way to do it that involves lighting a candle. Sound simple? It is—in part. Candle spells can be as simple or as complex as you would like, which leaves a lot of room for flexibility and creativity when choosing how to craft them. In the following sections, I will review candle color correspondences and how to dress and anoint candles as well as candle types and using candles for divination. I will also include a few of my own candle spells as well—but as always, I encourage you to create your own.

types of candles

Learning witchcraft comes with a lot of trial and error, but our practice does not start to evolve and grow until we branch out and start creating our own spells. Candle magick is a wonderful place to start due to its simplicity. Remember: It is your magick, and it must have you in it. You are the fundamental source in all that you will create, so grab some candles, get out there, and make some mistakes! To begin, here is a list of different types of candles and their magickal uses.

Birthday candles: These tiny, colorful candles are about 2.5 inches tall and 0.2 inches in diameter. While they are typically used to adorn birthday cakes, they're good for so much more. Birthday candles are perfect for the on-the-go witch, and they can be included in a travel altar or used in a spell you hope to manifest quickly. You can use the color correspondences in this chapter to align these candles (and all other candle types) with your intentions.

Chime candles: These small, convenient candles come in many colors and are typically 4 inches tall and 0.5 inches in diameter. These candles require either a small chime candle holder or a bed of salt to stay upright, but their quick burning time and wide array of available colors makes them a popular choice.

Figure candles: Figure candles cover a lot of ground. These can be in any shape the candlemaker desires, ranging from basic shapes like a heart to the form of Hekate. These candles make good devotional candles and altar adornments. However, due to their intricacy, you might consider them too pretty or too sacred to burn, but that is all right. They can still have their place on altars. There they can still be a representation of the fire element as well as whatever shape they have embodied.

Jar candles: You can find jar candles in a wide variety of colors and containers, which means the size of these candles can vary greatly. What makes a candle a jar candle is, quite literally, the fact that it is in a jar. There are no other prerequisites other than that. These candles are convenient because the wax collects within the container, and how long these candles will burn depends on the size of the jars.

Pillar candles: Pillar candles can come in a few different shapes, though they are often cylindrical and between 2 to 4 inches wide. These candles are large and burn for a long period of time. These are unlike jar candles in that they are freestanding. These candles are not burned in a jar and will need to be placed on a flat surface, such as a glass plate, to collect their wax drippings.

Seven-day candles: These candles are often around 8 inches tall and roughly 2.5 inches in diameter. Like their jar candle counterparts, they also come encased in glass. These candles are designed to be burned for a period of seven days. They are also referred to as novenas and have roots in the Catholic Church. As such, many times, depending on the religion or practice, you will see saints, gods, and goddesses printed on the front of these candles, and these days, the variety of such is growing. I have even seen a Saint Stevie Nicks candle appear on my timeline, and I don't disagree with the assessment.

Taper candles: Taper candles are often smaller candles in width that come in a large variety of colors. These candles are cylindrical in shape and taper to a smaller point at the top. While the lengths of these candles can vary, they're usually no more than 1 inch in diameter. Since these candles are often larger than chime candles, there is more room for detailed inscriptions and a larger area for dressing the candles. These candles will likely burn over a longer period of time than chime candles too.

Tealight candles: These candles are small, round candles affixed to metal containers of a similar size. These candles are about 0.5 inches tall and 1.5 inches wide. Due to their size, they have a quick burn and are great for spells you are working through quickly.

Votive candles: Votive candles are small, thick candles typically placed in small glass containers. The height of these candles vary, but they are typically no wider than 1.5 inches, and the containers for these candles are usually sold separately. These can be confused with tealight candles, but the difference between the two is that votive candles can be separated from their containers before they are burned, and votives are slightly larger than tealights.

CANDLE COLORS

As with crystals and herbs, colors also have their own correspondences. By knowing what the common color associations are, we can increase the specificity of our spells by coordinating our intentions with the colors. That said, I also believe in following our intuition. While this list is a great starting point, if you personally associate a certain color with a certain attribute, you can easily make that a part of your individualized practice. Some candle colors may be harder to find than others, and white candles make a great substitution.

Black: Baneful magick, banishing, binding, endings, forgiveness, grief, overcoming obstacles, protection, and releasing

Blue: Calmness, communication, confidence, creativity, forgiveness, fortune, healing, loyalty, peace, protection, success, and wisdom

Brown: Balance, endurance, justice, money, protection, success, and wealth

Dark blue: Depression, emotions, healing, meditation, peace, protection, the subconscious, and truth

Gold: Achievements, attraction, confidence, fast action, fortune, healing, prosperity, recognition, victory, wealth, and winning

Gray: Astral travel, competition, compromise, invisibility, neutralizing, and processing emotions

Green: Abundance, ambition, business matters, growth, healing, jealousy, luck, money, and success

Light blue: Harmony, healing, patience, peace, psychic enhancement, tranquility, and understanding

Orange: Attraction, business, confidence, creativity, energy, happiness, justice, legal matters, luck, and power

Pink: Affection, attraction, compassion, friendship, harmony, reconciliation, romance, and trust

Purple: Astral travel, divination, influence, past-life work, power, progress, protection, psychic enhancement, tranquility, and wisdom

Red: Career, courage, energy, fast action, health, lust, passion, protection, sex magick, strength, and willpower

Silver: Astral projection, divination, intuition, meditation, psychic enhancement, repelling negativity, and success

Violet: Blessings, intuition, psychic enhancement, self-improvement, spiritual growth, and success

White: Creativity, divination, meditation, protection, purity, spirituality, substitution, truth, and youth

Yellow: Change, confidence, creativity, focus, hope, inspiration, intelligence, joy, logic, memory, mental clarity, and travel

CLeansing

It is a good practice to cleanse any object or tool that you use for spiritual work, and candles are no exception. There are several methods available, but the most common is likely smoke cleansing, and you can use a variety of different herb bundles to cleanse your candles before their use. You could also use incense, such as frankincense or myrrh, to cleanse your candle before your ritual. If you would like, you can also use charged or blessed water, but you would need to ensure that the wick has properly dried before performing your candle spell. These are hardly the only methods a practitioner can use for cleansing, and you are encouraged to explore and develop other methods as you personalize your practice.

DRESSING AND ANOINTING

Dressing and anointing are phrases you will hear around the community, and they are sometimes used interchangeably or paired together. Dressing is the act of placing herbs and oils on your candle that align with its specific purpose. For a list of herb correspondences, refer to chapter 9. Anointing, by definition, is to ritually smear or rub down an object with a particular substance, typically an oil, but it can also be any "substance." This can also include the process of inscription, which I will go over next. In short, anointing is the act of preparing your candle for the full ritual, whereas dressing your candle typically means placing herbs and oils on it. These are two important parts of the candle magick process, but they are not by any means "necessary." Candle magick can be as simple as lighting a candle and focusing your will and intention on the outcome as it burns.

INSCRIPTION

Inscriptions are a great way to personalize your candle magick with your specific intention. Inscriptions can be made with a dedicated tool, or you can use common items, such as a toothpick or a thumbtack, to perform the action. There are not any rules specifying which object you must use, and as long as it gets the job done, it's allowed. Inscriptions can be planetary symbols or runes, words, phrases, or even your own personal sigils that you have created that are unique to you and your intentions.

Sigils

While I do not personally use sigils often in my practice, they're popular symbols used when inscribing candles. A sigil is a symbol that is created by you that represents a mantra or intention. There are helpful methods for sigil creation that can be found in books and on the internet, but you are not limited by them.

Perhaps a symbol has come to you in a dream, or you've created a sigil by the use of automatic writing. These sigils are just as valid as sigils created using any other method. Let your intuition guide you. Once you have created your sigil, imbue it with its meaning, and then it is good to go. You can inscribe your sigil on candles, draw it in your makeup, or drizzle it in your coffee using creamer or in your tea with honey. Anything goes.

Runes

As I am not an avid sigil user, my candle spells typically involve the use of words or symbols. Instead of sigils, I borrow symbols from runes. Runes are letters or symbols that were used largely in Scandinavian countries. The first discovery of runes was thought to have been around 160 CE, and it was made in Denmark.[65] Whether runes were used as divination or merely a lettering system has been much debated, but most studies approach runes as the former. In modern times, the practice of rune casting is utilized as a method of divination as each symbol is associated with certain correspondences. The twenty-four elder futhark runes are as follows:

ᚠ	**Fehu:** Financial security, good luck, new beginnings, prosperity, success, and travel
ᚢ	**Uruz:** Breakthroughs, courage, health, luck, overcoming obstacles, strength, and vitality
ᚦ	**Thurisaz:** Conflict, overcoming challenges, passion, protection, and regeneration

---

65. Groeneveld, "Runes."

ᚦ	**Ansuz:** Artistic endeavors, communication, inspiration, intellect, and transformation
ᚱ	**Raidho:** Growth, initiative, justice, rationality, relocation, and successful journeys
ᚲ	**Kenaz:** Creativity, fertility, inspiration, new information, and solutions
ᚷ	**Gebo:** Commitment, contracts, forgiveness, generosity, and harmonious relationships
ᚹ	**Wunjo:** Achievements, contentment, fulfillment, harmony, joy, and optimism
ᚺ	**Hagalaz:** Inner harmony, objective confrontations, positive transformations, and temporary disruptions
ᚾ	**Nauthiz:** Celebration, development, personal success, reigniting passions, and self-reliance

ᛁ	**Isa:** Preparation, reconciliation, self-control, and slow progress
ᛁ	**Jera:** Fertility, peace, promotions, and rewards
ᛇ	**Eihwaz:** Endurance, friendship, initiation, loyalty, love, new beginnings, and resourcefulness
ᛈ	**Pertho:** Fellowship, good omens, recognizing patterns, standing up for beliefs, and unexpected fortune
ᛉ	**Algiz:** Altruism, awakenings, connection, fulfilling dreams, and protection
ᛋ	**Sowilo:** Fame, fortune, guidance, happiness, health, hope, self-confidence, and travel
ᛏ	**Tiwaz:** Faith, justice, long-term travel, rationality, self-sacrifice, truth, and victory

ᛒ	**Berkano:** Fertility, healing, life changes, regeneration, and renewal
ᛗ	**Ehwaz:** Balance, harmonious relationships, joint ventures, negotiations, relocation, and teamwork
ᛗ	**Mannaz:** Acceptance, awareness, equality, intellect, learning, rational mind, social order, structure, and sustainability
ᛚ	**Laguz:** Astral plane, dreams, flow states, intuition, opportunities, psychic powers, taking risks, trusting self, and the unconscious mind
◇	**Inguz:** Fertility, growth, love, personal development, sex magick, and wholeness
ᛟ	**Othala:** Emotional stability, financial stability, freedom, happy home, and improved health
ᛞ	**Dagaz:** Awakening, believing in self, enlightenment, good fortune, new beginnings, and transmutations

Witchcraft in Action
HeaLtH canDLe speLL

I use the term *health* to mean both mental and physical health, and this spell can be used for either. If you or a loved one are in need of a little extra assistance, this is a spell you can use to attract healing. Please note that this is not a suitable replacement for therapy or consulting with a professional.

Materials:
*   Inscription tool, such as a thumbtack or toothpick
*   Black or white chime candle (for banishing)
*   Green or blue chime candle (for healing)
*   Patchouli, frankincense, or sandalwood essential oil (for banishing)
*   Eucalyptus, rosemary, pine, or juniper essential oil (for healing)
*   Lighter or matches

Directions:
1. Use the inscription tool to inscribe the candles with what you hope to banish on the black or white candle and what you hope to attract on the blue or green candle. If you have a sigil you would like to use, you can inscribe the candles with it, or you can simply write "health" on your blue or green candle and "negativity" on your black or white candle.

2. Rub the banishing oil of choice on the black or white candle and the healing oil on the green or blue candle. When anointing my candles, I rub from bottom to top to banish and from top to bottom to attract, but the method is up to you. What is most important is that your intentions are clear. And always remember: safety first. While oils are included here, remember that they are flammable, and remember to use a minimal amount when anointing your candles. If you would like, you can skip this step altogether. Either way, do not leave your candles unattended once lit.

3. Raise your energy in the method that works for you, such as dancing or channeling energy from external sources.

4. Once you are in the right headspace, light both candles.

5. While the candles burn down, focus on what you are releasing and what you are drawing forth. The candles themselves are enchanting and allow you to become immersed in your focus. Lean into this and channel your will as you work while the candles burn down.

Witchcraft in Action
BANISHING CANDLE SPELL

At times in your life, you will have something you need to release. This could be a person, a bad habit, or baggage that you are no longer willing to carry. This simple spell is to aid you in releasing whatever it is that is no longer needed. Since this is a banishing spell, it is best performed under a Waning Moon. However, if it cannot wait, it does not need to.

This spell is written with instructions to write whatever it is you wish to release on bay leaves. If you do not have bay leaves on hand, pieces of paper will work in their place. Alternatively, you can write what you are releasing directly onto the surface of the candle. What is most important is focusing on what you are releasing.

Materials:
* Black or white chime candle (for banishing)
* Permanent marker
* Bay leaves
* Pair of tweezers or tongs
* Lighter or matches
* Firesafe dish

Directions:
1. Write what you hope to release on the bay leaves. Use as many bay leaves as there are things you wish to release.

2. Light the candle.

3. Use tongs or tweezers to hold your bay leaves individually and place them into the flame, lighting them on fire. As the bay leaves burn, hold them over the firesafe dish.

4. Once you have burned through what you wish to release and the candle has burned down, dispose of the ashes away from you.

Witchcraft in Action
Happiness Candle Spell

If you need to invite more positivity and happiness into your life, this is a spell you can use. However, much like the Health Candle Spell, this is not meant to be a substitute for medical care. There are times when magick alone is not enough, and while this spell has served me well, mental health is of utmost importance. Magick cannot take the place of professional help if it is necessary; we must recognize when our problems are too large for us to carry on our own and seek help when needed. This spell would be best performed under a Waxing Moon to draw happiness toward you.

Materials:
* Orange or yellow chime candle (for vitality and energy)
* Inscription tool, such as a thumbtack or toothpick
* Ylang-ylang, orange, or grapefruit essential oil (for happiness)
* Lighter or matches

Directions:
1. On the surface of the candle, inscribe the word "happiness," a personal sigil, or the rune symbol for Wunjo.

2. Anoint the candle with the oil. While I have suggested a few oils in the materials list, you can reference the essential oil list in chapter 9 for other prospects. Whatever oil you use, remember to use it sparingly as oils can be flammable.

3. Light the candle and focus on attracting joy and happiness into your life while simultaneously sloughing off the daily grind and problems that have been accumulating in your life. They add up quickly, and they must be let go of to maintain a healthy stasis.

4. While the candle burns, breathe in the energy and feel the changes taking place within until the candle has burned down.

Witchcraft in Action
fresh start candle spell

This candle spell is for when you are in need of a new beginning or a fresh start. This is necessary when you feel as if you have been stagnant for too long or dislike your current trajectory. In short, this candle spell is done to usher in a new era for you. This spell is best done during a New Moon or a Waxing Moon.

Materials:
* Green or white chime candle (for new beginnings)
* Peppermint or frankincense essential oil (for a fresh start)
* Permanent marker
* Paper
* Lighter or matches
* Tweezer or tongs
* Firesafe dish

Directions:
1. Once you've gathered your materials, anoint your candle with the essential oil of choice. Remember, use this oil sparingly!

2. Use the marker to write down your intentions on the paper. Be specific. What would you like to see more of in your life? What would you like to see less of? Write this down.

3. Once you have written down your intentions, light your candle.

4. Hold the paper with tweezer or tongs and light it with the candle's fire to activate your desires.

5. Hold the burning paper over the firesafe dish, and focus your attention on both your intentions and your energy, projecting them outward into the universe. While watching your intentions burn, visualize the message flowing from you into the universe. Sit with the gratitude that they will arrive to you soon as the candle burns down.

Broom Closet Witch Tips

Candles make yet another practice that is easy to conceal as they're handy for power outages and are frequently included in emergency kits, and it is rather common to find at least one decorative candle in a home. These candles come in a variety of shapes, sizes, and colors that you can use for different workings. I frequently pick up black candles in musky scents, such as "Warm Pipe Tobacco," and light them in my home as a method of cleansing and protection. Using color correspondences makes for an easy way to channel these energies in your workings.

Of course, this practice doesn't have to be extensive. White candles make excellent substitutes for any other colored candle a practitioner might need, so your collection doesn't have to be expansive to be efficient.

But what if we're renting or otherwise aren't allowed to burn items in our homes? We can use LED candles to supplement a candle in our workings. This may not be the most traditional of methods, but it is a valid way to perform the ceremony without breaking the terms of your lease agreement.

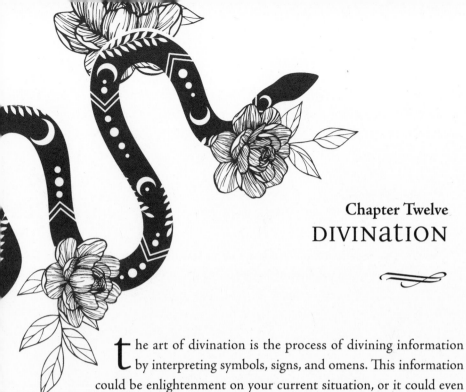

Chapter Twelve

DIVINATION

t he art of divination is the process of divining information by interpreting symbols, signs, and omens. This information could be enlightenment on your current situation, or it could even assist you in predicting future outcomes. The methods of divination vary, and in this chapter, I will cover some of the most popular forms. Please note that divination does not have to be a part of your practice, but it is a helpful tool in deciphering both ourselves and the world around us.

Keep in mind that divination is an art that takes practice. When performing divination, it is wise to record what you see, how it feels, and how it might apply to your life. I recommended writing this information down in your Book of Shadows or a notebook used specifically for this purpose. There are times when messages will not make sense in the moment, but when we view them in hindsight, we can make the connections that we were unable to at first. This is a process, and it takes time. By keeping a journal of your practices, you can reference previous readings and notice key elements you may have missed initially.

CANDLE DIVINATION

Candle divination is a useful and inexpensive method of divination that can be performed in unison with your candle magick. This type of divination is also quite versatile as there are a few different methods that you can utilize in your practice. Some of the most popular methods of candle divination are ceromancy (*wax reading*), pyromancy (*flame reading*), and capnomancy (*smoke reading*).

Ceromancy: Wax Reading

Ceromancy is the art of reading your candle wax. This can be done once your candle magick has been completed, and it is particularly useful if the pattern of wax is unusual versus a solid pool melted on the bottom of the plate. However, this method of divination can also be performed by letting melted wax drop into water or onto a plate. To interpret your candle wax, you must observe the patterns that you see both in the wax shapes themselves as well as the negative space between them.

While some people and publications believe that there can be set meanings to particular shapes, it is my own belief that symbolism is deeply personal. Although there are some interpretations that can be similar among people, a person typically views things through their own lens. An example of this would be if, in your wax, you see the image of a snake. While one person might believe this to be a symbol of transformation and grace, another person, who is terrified of snakes, might view this as ominous—and both interpretations can be correct. What matters the most is that you are considering your own working knowledge and emotions about what you are viewing. By doing so, you can apply this information to the interpretation of the wax itself. Ask yourself not only *what* it is that you are seeing but *how you feel* about what it is you are seeing. This is not exclusive to reading candle wax, either. This analysis is also helpful in dream interpretation and scrying, among other things.

Pyromancy: Flame Reading

Pyromancy is the art of reading your candle flame while you are performing candle magick. While influences on the type of flame that appears can be structural in nature, you can also view the flame as an indication of your spell's performance.

Dancing: If your flame is moving rhythmically, it can be a good indication! A dancing flame is seen as communication and as a sign that your spell is working out in your favor.

Disappearing: If your flame extinguishes during your workings with no known cause, this is a sign that something is interfering with your magick. It can also be an indication that it is not the proper time for your spell.

Double: If there are two separate flames present, you will have to pay attention to their interaction to discern the meaning. If they are dancing in unison with one another, it could be a sign that your workings will be successful. However, if they seem to be competing, it could be an indication of resistance.

Flickering: A flickering flame is a sign that there is something working against your spellwork and that there may be chaotic energy surrounding your workings.

Inconsistent: If your flame varies between strong, weak, or other attributes, it can be an indication that there may be obstruction within your workings or that your spell may only partially work.

Noisy: If a flame is hissing or making other audible noises, it is an indication that something is trying to communicate with you. What this communication might be is heavily reliant on the type of spellwork you are performing, be mindful of the sound's tone and your own feelings about what you are hearing.

Strong: A strong, steady flame is considered a good sign! If your flame is consistent, this can be an indication of successful spellwork.

Weak: A weak flame can be an indication of a blockage in your spellwork and a call for you to channel more energy into your workings so the spellwork will materialize.

Capnomancy: Smoke Reading

Capnomancy is the art of reading smoke, but it is not exclusive to candle magick and the smoke your candle emits. You can also do this when you are smoke cleansing with herb bundles or incense. With candle magick, there can be physical reasons for smoke, such as additional herbs, but you can still discern what is being communicated through the smoke in a number of ways. You can interpret the shapes you see as well as the color of the smoke and the direction the smoke is moving. If you are working with container candles, you can also interpret the soot that is left behind in the jar to seek out hidden messages. At times there can be messages shared either literally through words or symbolically through shapes.

When reading smoke during candle magick, you must pay attention to the signs. If there is excessive candle smoke, it can be an indication of forces working against you and a sign that the spell may not manifest in the way it was intended. The direction of the smoke can have meaning, too, but there are nuances in this that you must consider, such as the type of spellwork you are performing. For instance, smoke moving toward you while performing baneful magick would have an entirely different meaning than if you were performing a prosperity spell. This is because the symbolism in smoke moving toward you is exactly that—whatever you are working toward is coming toward you. The reverse can be true if the candle smoke is moving away from you.

cartomancy

Cartomancy is another form of divination that uses a deck of cards to foresee the future or help provide perspective. There are several different types of decks that a person can use. Out of all these decks, the tarot is perhaps the most popular, but this isn't your only option if you're looking to explore this method of divination.

Oracle

While tarot cards are more structured, oracle cards can vary from deck to deck. Typically there are somewhere between thirty to seventy cards in each deck. What each deck includes artistically and throughout the text is solely up to the creator, which means that each deck will have a theme unique to the creator. As such, each new oracle deck is an opportunity to learn the language of those particular cards. Remember that it will take time to bond with and learn each distinctive deck. Many individuals prefer this less traditional structure as it can feel less intimidating.

Often, oracle cards are thought of as the kinder kin to tarot. While tarot messages can be more direct, oracle cards are more often geared toward inspiration and encouragement. An oracle deck's purpose is to increase your intuition and connection with yourself through their use. The user must connect with the imagery of the cards and, as such, should pick a deck they are most drawn to. Oracle cards can be read in a variety of spreads, but they're also great to use for one-card pulls, which is when you simply pull a single card and read it as a daily reading. Creators of these decks will include suggested spreads in the guidebooks that come with the decks, but you can even combine oracle card readings with other methods of divination to create a truly unique experience for yourself.

Lenormand

Lenormand cards are another option for individuals wanting to practice cartomancy. These decks include thirty-six cards with corresponding images, such as a clover, a key, clouds, and a tree. Each of these cards represents themes that may be occurring in our lives or have yet to appear. Lenormand cards are often read in pairs with the cards' own intricacies being layered with the other cards in the spread. In pairing the cards, we are able to refine their meaning and apply them to situations and outcomes with greater detail.

Lenormand Cards

1. **The Rider:** Action, forward motion, messages, and news
2. **The Clover:** Encouragement, good fortune, luck, and positivity
3. **The Ship:** Changes, journeys, opportunities, and travel
4. **The House:** Home, sanctuary, security, and stability
5. **The Tree:** Growth, internal strength, traditions, and wisdom
6. **The Clouds:** Change, confusion, issues surfacing, and uncertainty
7. **The Snake:** Deception, hidden enemies, regeneration, and seduction
8. **The Coffin:** Death, endings, grief, and loss
9. **The Bouquet:** Appreciation, happiness, positivity, and romance
10. **The Scythe:** Clearing, endings, growth, and warnings
11. **The Whip:** Arguments, opposition, unrest, and wrath
12. **The Birds:** Broadcasting, communication, gossip, and intuition
13. **The Child:** Beginnings, children, honesty, and innocence
14. **The Fox:** Caution, cunning, suspicion, and trickery
15. **The Bear:** Authority, business, instinct, and power
16. **The Star:** Assessments, inspiration, positivity, and visions
17. **The Stork:** Deliverance, gifts, news, and transitions
18. **The Dog:** Companionship, dependency, loyalty, and obedience
19. **The Tower:** Defense, established systems, isolation, and objectivity
20. **The Garden:** Networking, socializing, society, and unions
21. **The Mountains:** Blocks, inflexibility, obstacles, and stubbornness

22. **The Ways:** Choices, decisions, opportunities, and travel

23. **The Mice:** Lacking resources, loss, missed details, and unraveling

24. **The Heart:** Harmony, love, relationships, and support

25. **The Ring:** Being stuck, bonds, commitment, and contracts

26. **The Book:** Knowledge, research, secrets, and wisdom

27. **The Letter:** Documents, communication, expression, and invitations

28. **The Gentleman:** Assertion, masculine energy, and masculinity

29. **The Lady:** Feminine energy, femininity, and nurturing

30. **The Lily:** Fertility, passion, purity, and sexuality

31. **The Sun:** Success, victory, warmth, and well-being

32. **The Moon:** Creativity, cycles, emotions, and reactivity

33. **The Key:** Doors opening, opportunity, revelation, and unlocking

34. **The Fish:** Capital, change of tides, hidden truths, and resources

35. **The Anchor:** Hope, restraint, stability, and vocation

36. **The Cross:** Finality, restrictions, sacrifice, and struggle

Tarot

Tarot cards are another great divination tool. These decks have a set number of seventy-eight cards as they are structured, even among varying decks, and I will go over the common themes of these cards as a base point reference for beginners. If you are a seasoned reader, feel free to skip this section as it will not be covering new ground. For beginners, there are a variety of different spreads you can try out, but I recommend starting with a daily one-card pull to familiarize yourself with the cards as you learn. Once you select the card, allow yourself to take in the imagery of the card and evaluate how it makes you feel. Take the time to jot down the card you pulled, your interpretation, your feelings about the card, and how it applies to your life. This practice will assist you in learning the cards and strengthening your connection with your subconscious.

Major Arcana

The major arcana cards are the first twenty-two cards in the tarot deck, beginning with the number zero and ending at twenty-one. These cards are representative of major themes in our lives, and they are often the most recognizable cards in the deck. Think of these cards as the big picture cards as each one covers an archetype. The themes of these cards can be applied to our lives to deepen our understanding of both our external and internal worlds.

0. **The Fool:** Beginnings, carelessness, innocence, spontaneity, and trust

1. **The Magician:** Action, confidence, creativity, sleight of hand, and willpower

2. **The High Priestess:** Divine femininity, intuition, spirituality, and wisdom

3. **The Empress:** Abundance, creativity, fertility, maternal energy, and nurturing

4. **The Emperor:** Ambition, authority, paternal energy, stability, and structure

5. **The Hierophant:** Assertive, conformity, education, mentor, and morality

6. **The Lovers:** Companionship, love, and optimism,

7. **The Chariot:** Control, self-assertion, triumph, victory, and will

8. **Strength:** Compassion, fortitude, power, self-control, and strength

9. **The Hermit:** Caution, guidance, introspection, searching, and solitude

10. **Wheel of Fortune:** Destiny, luck, success, turning points, and visions

11. **Justice:** Balance, decisions, justice, repercussions, and responsibility

12. **The Hanged Man:** Letting go, reversals, sacrifice, and suspensions

13. **Death:** Change, eliminations, endings, transformations, and transitions

14. **Temperance:** Balance, health, middle path, moderation, and temperance

15. **The Devil:** Addictions, hopelessness, ignorance, and materialism

16. **The Tower:** Catastrophe, release, revelations, and sudden changes

17. **The Star:** Faith, generosity, hope, inspiration, and rejuvenation

18. **The Moon:** Fear, illusions, imagination, intuition, and unconscious

19. **The Sun:** Assurance, celebration, enlightenment, success, and vitality

20. Judgment: Awakening, judgment, rebirth, reflection, and realizations

21. The World: Accomplishments, completion, fulfillment, and harmony

Minor Arcana

The minor arcana makes up the remaining fifty-six cards in the tarot deck. If the major arcana is the big picture, think of the minor arcana as the details. One of the simplest ways to master tarot, outside of reading symbolism within the cards themselves, is to have a working knowledge of the suits as well as the numbers and their individual meanings. Knowing these pieces helps you in bringing the picture together, which then allows you to interpret the meaning more readily.

Suits

Pentacles: Pentacles are attributed to the element of earth, and this suit corresponds with the signs of Taurus, Virgo, and Capricorn.

Common themes: Finances, material world, and practical matters

Swords: Swords are related to the element of air, and these cards are associated with the signs of Gemini, Libra, and Aquarius.

Common themes: Challenges, ideas, and matters of the mind

Wands: Wands are associated with the element of fire and the signs of Aries, Leo, and Sagittarius.

Common themes: Actions, motivation, passions, and purpose

Cups: Cups are attributed to the element of water and associated with the signs of Cancer, Scorpio, and Pisces.

Common themes: Emotions, matters of the heart, and relationships

Court Cards

When the court cards appear in a reading, they can represent people or influences in our lives or aspects of ourselves. To determine their meaning, you must reflect on the overarching theme of the spread in its entirety to see how it applies to your life. Like each suit, each court card has common themes.

Kings: Kings represent the final card in the minor arcana, and with this, there is an emphasis on success, completion, and fulfillment. They are of the highest status in the minor arcana.

Common themes: Authority, the external, leadership, masculinity, and maturity

Queens: The queen is a card that also sits at the top of the minor arcana. She has reached peak maturity and has confidence in her abilities. The queens are the feminine counterpart to the masculine influences of the kings.

Common themes: Creativity, femininity, internal, leadership, and maturity

Knights: While knights are considered to have experience under their belts, they are not at the level of maturity found in both the kings and queens. However, they are a devoted court card, and with this, they have attributes of dedication and follow-through. This card can present itself more erratically than the previous two court cards, though.

Common themes: Action, dedication, energy, extremist, and journeys

Page: Pages sit at the bottom of the court cards, and with this, they are considered less mature than the kings, queens, and knights. They bring an air of energy and youth to their pursuits. These cards are in the initial phases of personal development and growth.

Common themes: Beginnings, discovery, energy, learning, and youth

Card Numbers

Aces: Action, beginnings, decisions, opportunities, and potential

Twos: Balance, collaboration, duality, opposition, and partnerships

Threes: Action, change, creativity, groups, and growth

Fours: Boredom, manifesting, stability, stagnation, and structure

Fives: Changes, conflict, instability, struggles, and unknowns

Sixes: Cooperation, harmony, realignment, reconciliation, and restorations

Sevens: Assessment, knowledge, reflection, solutions, and understanding

Eights: Achievement, action, advancing, change, and success

Nines: Attainment, fruition, fulfillment, mastery, and transitions

Tens: Closure, completion, culmination, endings, and renewal

SPIRIT BOARDS

I have been fond of spirit boards since I got my first in the late '90s. It was a glorious glow-in-the-dark Parker Brothers Ouija board, and I was absolutely enchanted. To be clear, I had no idea what I was doing. I was a kid, and my frontal lobe had not fully developed. But that did not stop my love and appreciation of these boards. These boards are sometimes (in my opinion) unfairly given a bad rep, but what hasn't been when it comes to the occult and the unknown?

Spirit boards, or talking boards, are commonly referred to as Ouija boards, which was a name that was adopted from the first mass-market versions of these boards. However, talking boards have been around for much longer than the trademarked Ouija, and as such, talking board is the generic name for the device. The boards themselves primarily have the alphabet printed atop along with simple answers, such as yes and no, and you navigate this board with the assistance of the planchette, a small heart-shaped object that typically has a hole or window in the center for reading. Some planchettes lack this detail, and you would read the letter the tip of the planchette points at rather than the one shown in the center.

The planchette itself is moved ever so slightly around the board by our fingertips until coming to a stop over the letters or numbers. The mundane explanation for this is that we are simply moving the planchette ourselves. Sure, but this isn't the full scope. Depending on the intentions for using the board, we can communicate with the spirits around us or divine messages from our higher selves or spirit guides.

While spirit boards are a divinatory tool, they are often shrouded in cautionary tales. The tool itself isn't more ominous than another method. Rather, this notoriety is more likely due to a person being able to purchase one in the toy section of their local big-box store. Children and adults alike can set out to summon spirits without knowing how or why. This does not lend its hand to a person using discretion or protection when attempting to use this item, and both are necessary. I discussed protections in chapter 2, and you will need to make use of them before using a spirit board as a divination tool. When using this device, you will want to be specific about the type of energies you are hoping to communicate with. The last thing you want is to open a Grand Central Station portal directly in your living room, so setting boundaries beforehand is a pivotal step in the process.

Before even using the board, you must set the stage. You will want to cleanse your room, light candles for protection, and create an energetic boundary, either by formally casting a circle or informally creating an energetic barrier. Use whatever you are most comfortable with and has shown to be most effective in your practice. You must be specific as to what or whom you wish to communicate with when using this board. This can be done audibly after you have cleansed your space and set up boundaries. Let it be known what or whom you are attempting to make contact with and that you would like to exclude other spirits that may be present from this session. If you have a photograph of the particular person you hope to interact with, place it nearby. Allow yourself to get into a meditative-like state and place your fingers on the planchette. As the planchette moves, keep a log of where the planchette has landed, both within the window and where the tip of the planchette lands. Once you have gathered this information, you can make sense of it after the fact. Often the letters appear as a jumbled mess, and you will have to decode what the intended message is.

If you notice the energy has shifted in your home or believe something is lingering after your session, cleanse your space thoroughly. While I have not had this experience with a spirit board, I have had a spirit unwilling to leave my residence a time or two before. I prefer to blend a few methods of protection to make sure the spirit knows that I mean business. Unless they intend to split utilities with me, they are no longer an invited presence in my abode.

In this situation, I use a protective herb bundle and cleanse my house while leaving the doors open. Once I have cleansed each room, I focus on doorways and audibly request that the spirit leave the premises. If the energy is still off, I go through with my banishing spray, which is included in chapter 2. Afterward, I will sit with myself in a form of meditation that allows me to clearly project my energetic boundaries around the circumference of my home. As discussed previously, this presents itself as a light, and specifically when creating boundaries, it is a circle of light around my entire body. Through meditation and visualization, I increase the size until my home is within the confines of the protective circle. While this typically holds for a good length of time, I do repeat this process as necessary.

PENDULUMS

A pendulum is defined as a weighted object that is attached to the end of a chain or cord. A pendulum can be made from many different materials, such as crystal, metal, wood, and glass, but never a magnetic material, as it can skew your interpretations. Each material used to create a pendulum comes with its own energy.

Crystal pendulums carry their own frequencies, and these are in relation to the properties of the crystals themselves. Clear quartz can be a good option for a vast array of properties due to the open nature of the crystal. It is a stone that amplifies energies and also cleanses and balances. If you have a specific purpose for your pendulum, you can seek out a crystal that aligns with the intent.

Metal pendulums can include brass, copper, silver, and gold. Due to the nature of their composition, these materials are conductors and therefore more receptive to subtle energies. There is an argument on each side of the coin for this. Some people believe metal pendulums to be better for this reason, whereas others believe their responsiveness to all energies interferes with their purpose.

Wood, which is the least conductive material used for pendulums, is sometimes preferred because it is not affected by outside energies. Wood pendulums are only receptive to the energy of the person holding the item.

You should select your pendulum based on your own individual preferences. Use your intuition to guide you to the energy you would prefer to work with.

Once you have your pendulum, the first thing you should do with it—and any tools that you choose to work with—is to cleanse it. This can be achieved by submerging it in running water, using sunlight or moonlight, performing a smoke cleanse, or utilizing a saltwater bath. Periodically your pendulum will need to be cleansed again to get rid of energies that accumulated. You can do this routinely, cleansing before each use, or you can cleanse your pendulum when you feel that you are not connecting with it. Be mindful of the material of your pendulum when choosing a method to cleanse it.

The next step is to program your pendulum. Clear your mind and hold the chain of your pendulum between your thumb and index finger until the pendulum stops swinging. Once your pendulum is still, ask it simple yes or no questions that you know the answers to. This will help you gauge your pendulum's responses. A pendulum can move back and forth, side to side, or in a circular motion. As you ask the questions, record the answers and the pendulum's corresponding motions. It is important to find out how your pendulum responds so you can use it accordingly.

Pendulums are best for yes or no answers. Use them to help connect to your higher self to determine questions that can be answered using these simple responses. While pendulums can be used for more detailed questions, be prepared to recite a dissertation to get to your final answer (unless you are using a pendulum mat or a mat that includes specific answers or even the alphabet for long answers).

SCRYING

Scrying can be done on a multitude of surfaces, but it typically means staring into a crystal ball, darkened mirror, water, or even fire, as I touched on in the previous section. Scrying is done to divine answers from the images you see reflected, and this method of divination, much like reading flames or wax, is heavily reliant on symbolism. In order to interpret your readings, you must first sit with what you are seeing and dig into what it means for you. This requires asking yourself how what you are seeing makes you feel and applying it back to your question or the situation you are attempting to seek answers for. Based on my own experience, there may be occasions when you intuit something that is separate from your inquiry altogether. It may, instead, be another message entirely or even a message for someone close to you. Keep an open mind when making sense of what you see.

While scrying is a wonderful art for divining the future, it is not a method that I regularly reference in my practice as I do not have the same connection to it that I do with other forms of divination. However, when testing the waters, it is good to try out different methods of divination to see which medium you connect with on a personal level, and your preferred methods may change over time, which is just fine. Your practice will likely not look the same now as it will in a few years, and that's a good thing. That is growth, and evolution is progress. When starting out, you do not need to be overly concerned with picking the proper method for you. Try out a medium and see how it feels. Record your findings so you can reflect on your readings, and you can then pinpoint what you've had the most success with as well as what you feel most connected to.

tHe "cLaIrs"

Some people do not need any tools at all when it comes to divining the future, and it is thought that these people have an aptitude for a type of clairvoyance. And this can be true. There are likely people who were born with the ability to access this sort of information more readily. However, what does not seem to be mentioned often enough is that it is possible for those of us who do not feel as if we were gifted from birth to hone and refine these senses. This type of intuition can be developed through practice, and yes, this is another practice that is heavily reliant on meditation. You must be able to sit within trance states and listen to the world around you to absorb the messages being given to you without interferences of doubt.

It is likely that you, yourself, have had the phone ring, and you knew who the person calling was going to be and what they needed to say before you ever glanced at your phone. Or perhaps you have dreamed of something, mundane as it may be, and had it happen afterward. There could have been times when you knew the answer to a question without rational explanation or understood someone's motivations without clear evidence. These are moments when we are keenly tuned into the intuition that surrounds us. These moments happen when we are operating on a plane that allows us to notice subtleties we might otherwise ignore.

There are several different methods of developing your intuition from which this sort of information can emerge. These are often referred to as the "clairs," and they each reference a different method of processing intuition. No one type is greater than the others, as they are simply different facets of processing the information that we receive when we are able to "tune in" to the specific frequency. There are some forms we may have more of a natural inclination to than others, but they can be developed. While other lists tend to include more variants, such as smell and taste, I will focus on the four main clairs.

Clairvoyance: "Clear Seeing"

Clairvoyance is the clair that gets the most airtime as it is frequently presented in movies and television as a flash of insight. This is because what clairvoyance refers to is the art of seeing, making it the easiest to display on the screen and perhaps the most sought-after form of clair senses. It can sometimes feel like the most tangible method as the individual is *seeing* what is to come in some shape, form, or fashion.

Clairaudience: "Clear Hearing"

This "clair" refers to hearing, and what the individual hears can be words, a song, or other sounds that provide messages in an auditory format. Please note that the voices heard will be ones of encouragement. If the voices are telling you to do harm, this is not clairaudience. This is a concern, and you must seek out medical care.

Clairsentient: "Clear Feeling"

This refers to "feeling" something that may not be easy to put into words. It is an inner knowing that is not accompanied by words or sounds, but rather, it is a gut feeling. You have likely experienced this if you've met someone and are automatically put off by their presence. This is also something that is experienced if you walk into a room and can sense the tension or the overall collective feeling permeating the air.

Claircognizant: "Clear Knowing"

This clair is similar to clairsentience in that it takes the form of an inner knowing, but it differs in that it is not a feeling but more of a direct download of information. Have you ever just "known" something without having all the facts? That falls under the category of claircognizance.

Broom Closet Witch Tips

Divination can be one of the harder elements of witchcraft to conceal, but thanks to technology, there are a lot of ways to practice it without leaving any physical evidence. There are apps that make use of tarot cards, runes, numerology, palmistry, astrology, and several other forms of divination that will only leave a digital marker. While some of the apps draw for you, others are guides on how to learn to read these forms of divination yourself.

If you're looking for tangible ways to conceal your practice, you can use an ordinary deck of playing cards in the place of tarot. This practice is referred to as cartomancy. Keep in mind there are only fifty-two cards in a standard deck. When using this method, the jokers need to be removed from the deck, and the major arcana and knights will not be represented. That said, you can still gain valuable insight by using a deck of playing cards. In this system, the spades are swords, hearts are cups, diamonds are pentacles, and the clubs are wands. Queens and kings will be represented in a regular card deck as such, and the jack can be likened to the page as they represent a young person at the beginning of their journey.

Another method of divination you can practice in secrecy is creating your own pendulum. This can be done with only two items: a string and a weight of some sort, such as a ring or a pendant. In a pinch, you can also use any necklace you have with a sturdy pendant.

Candle scrying and other methods of scrying can also be very discrete ways to practice divination without leaving behind any evidence of such.

Chapter Thirteen
astrology

a strology is a beautiful tool for learning more about ourselves and our psyche. Our natal chart, sometimes referred to as our birth chart, is a map of our personality and our mission in life. A natal chart is a blueprint of the location of the stars and planets at the exact time and geographical location of a person's birth. Your own natal chart creates a snapshot that you can use to see the strengths and challenges you may face throughout your lifetime.

I am an astrology enthusiast. While I have studied astrology since the late 1990s, I am still learning. This is mostly because I view every aspect of life as having an opportunity to continuously learn, and astrology is a complex topic that varies on tradition. There are three major systems of astrology: Western, Vedic, and Chinese. I will focus on Western astrology in this chapter as I am proficient in this system; it is the system that I work within my own practice. However, I encourage you to explore astrology as a whole to find out which system works best for you.

There are several websites where you can enter your birth date, time of birth, and birth location, and they will generate a full report with a fundamental analysis for you. Gone are the days of drawing your chart by hand. Hand drawing a chart requires the use of an ephemeris showing the position of celestial bodies for a time period, an atlas, a ton of math, and a steady hand. What a time to be alive! Once you have this information in hand, you can start exploring your chart in-depth. While "What's your sign?" is a common question, it is a superficial one as we are much more than our sun signs. We are a culmination of the planets and their locations at our time of birth. Let us first work through a basic understanding of the planets before moving into the duality of signs, houses, and aspects.

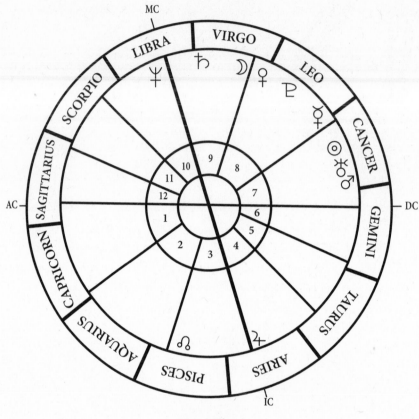

Natal Chart

I have selected the chart as an example because this chart is my big three twin, meaning we share each of these placements. Our "big three" consist of our ascendant, our sun, and our moon. There is also a "big six," which includes our ascendant, sun, moon, Mercury, Mars, and Venus. In this chart, you will see the ascendant is in Sagittarius, which begins the first house, the sun is in Cancer, the moon is in Virgo, Mercury is in Leo, Mars is in Cancer, and Venus is in Virgo. If this is confusing, don't worry. I will be going over this in more detail in this chapter.

pLanets

Planets are here to show us *what* energy is being expressed when we are interpreting our charts. Each planet has its own attributes, and these become the initial characters that create the story of us. Once you've collected your birth time, location, and date and input it into a chart generator, you will see that each of these planets is in a sign and house within your chart. But first, we must understand the energy of the planets themselves before we progress to understand what signs they are in and what domains they reside in.

Sun

Yes, this is not technically a planet—it is a star—but it's a fundamental part of our birth charts as well as our solar system. Its position at your time of birth determines which horoscope you will read in astrology articles for the better part of your life or, at the very least, until you deepen your understanding of astrology. The sun is what represents our inner world. This is our sense of self, and it's considered our basic personality. It is one component of what is referred to as our big three. The sun changes signs approximately every month.

Themes: Creativity, manifesting, self-expression, strength, and vitality

Sun Symbol

Moon

Equally as important as the sun (and also not a planet) is the moon. The moon is also a part of our big three and represents our emotions and how we process those emotions. The moon is our unconscious mind and our intuition at work. Whereas the sun is our surface expression of self, the moon's focus is our internal world. The sign the moon is in represents our temperament, and the moon's sign changes roughly every two to three days.

Themes: Compassion, emotions, imagination, intuition, and our unconscious mind

Moon Symbol

Ascendant

The ascendant, or rising sign, is also not a planet. Rather, it is the sign that is on the eastern horizon at your exact time of birth. This sign is quick moving and changes approximately every two hours. This is the final component of your "big three," and it is how you appear to the world, both physically and in your social personality. Some describe the ascendant as a "mask," but it is an integral part of your personality. This is the outmost expression of yourself, and it is the first impression you imprint upon someone when meeting them.

Themes: Appearance, impressions, and public persona

Ascendant Symbol

Mercury

Mercury is the planet of the mind and communication. This planet represents how we formulate our thoughts, the processes of our internal dialogue, how we learn, and how we communicate with others. While this is not a part of our big three, it is often included in the big six in astrology circles, which is a reference to our personal planets. Mercury is the closest planet to the sun and changes its sign approximately every three to four weeks.

Themes: Communication, intellect, knowledge, technology, and travel

Mercury Symbol

Venus

Venus is often considered the planet of love, and it shows us how we connect with others and form our relationships. Venus also governs finances, and the sign this planet is in can also be used to determine your relationship with money as well. The sign that Venus is in changes roughly every four to five weeks and is considered to be a part of your big six.

Themes: Attraction, beauty, finances, love, relationships, and romance

Venus Symbol

Mars

Mars represents your physical energy and drive, but the planet is not exclusive to physicality. Mars is considered the planet of action, and this presents itself as our driving force, our passions, and our aggression as well. Mars is also considered part of our big six, and the planet changes signs every six to seven weeks.

Themes: Action, aggression, drive, energy, and passion

Mars Symbol

Jupiter

Jupiter is the planet of luck and good fortune. Because of its distance from the sun, it is not considered a personal planet. Instead, it represents communal energy that is shared with our peers. Planets farther away from the sun are referred to as social planets, and they influence groups versus a singular person. When it comes to these planets, the houses they occur in become of particular importance. Jupiter is also a planet of philosophy, and it influences our spiritual views as well. This planet changes signs every twelve to thirteen months.

Themes: Expansion, fortune, growth, philosophy, and prosperity

$$\text{2}\!\!\!\downarrow$$

Jupiter Symbol

Saturn

Saturn is the planet of authority. This planet is farther from the sun than our personal planets, and because of this, it takes longer to move through signs. This makes Saturn a social planet as it affects those born around the same time period and is a representation of their collective karma. Saturn reflects our sense of discipline and structure, and it is also known as the planet of limitations. It shows where we will find the restrictions and obstacles within our own lives. As an outer planet, Saturn changes signs approximately every two to three years.

Themes: Authority, discipline, karma, responsibility, and sacrifice

Saturn Symbol

Uranus

Uranus is a planet of rebellion and is also referred to as the "Great Awakener." Due to its distance from the sun, Uranus is an outer planet and thus a generational planet. Uranus changes signs approximately every seven years. This is a planet that bucks the system, and it is one of innovation and originality. Its emphasis is on growth and forward motion, and it can show where a person can expect sudden changes or transformations within their life. With generational and transpersonal planets, we must pay attention to the houses these are placed in as well as the transits to see the overarching themes for our own lives. I will go over these shortly, but it is something to keep in mind!

Themes: Change, creation, eccentricity, freedom, and rebellion

Uranus Symbol

Neptune

Neptune is the planet of illusions and dreams. This is a planet that influences our creativity and our artistry. It is our inspiration and creative force that are powered by its dreamy mysticism. Neptune changes signs every ten to twelve years, which makes this a generational planet, and as such, we have to take into account its exact location on our birth charts and how it works with the other planets in our charts to determine how it manifests itself within our personal lives.

Themes: Illusion, imagination, inspiration, intuition, and vision

Neptune Symbol

Pluto

Pluto is the "planet" of death and rebirth, and it is the planet—though it is not classified as a planet any longer—that is known for its transformative energy. Pluto can be a dark, powerful influence, and it can highlight areas of obsession within our own lives. The sign that Pluto is in changes roughly every twelve to fifteen years, making it another one of the generational planets. Its location in your birth chart can determine its individual influence and areas in your life where you will face its regenerative power.

Themes: Death, power, rebirth, regeneration, and transformation

Pluto Symbol

SIGNS

While the planets tell us the energy, the signs tell us *how* that energy is expressed. The signs add an additional layer to the character of the planets, which gives each planet their own lens and depth. I will include the element each sign corresponds with as well as their modality. The modality can be either cardinal, fixed, or mutable. Cardinal signs kick off the seasons, and as such, they are the initiators of the zodiac. Fixed signs fall in the middle of the season and are stable but can be resistant to change, whereas mutable signs occur at the end of the season and are known for their adaptability. For the sake of being concise, I will break the signs apart by their strengths and their weaknesses so you can formulate your own overarching themes for these signs. Duality is an important facet of life and one that we should not shy away from. It exists in everything. Light and dark. Night and day. Strength and weakness. Above and below.

Aries

Element: Fire

Modality: Cardinal

Strengths: Brave, bold, courageous, driven, honest, independent, and self-assured

Weaknesses: Aggressive, careless, harsh, impatient, impulsive, selfish, and temperamental

Aries is the first sign of the zodiac, and thanks to this placement, it is the sign of beginnings and setting things in motion. Aries is represented by a ram and is ruled by the planet Mars. Aries is both a cardinal sign as well as a fire sign. Cardinal signs are the instigators of the zodiac, whereas fire signs are signs of action. This combination gives them a dynamic approach to life and their very own brand of diving into things head-on. All that fiery energy, passion, and ego can quickly come to a boiling point as this sign is not known for keeping its cool. While Aries can be described as "in your face," there is no lack of charisma and personality when it comes to this sign. They are aware of who they are and what they do or do not stand for.

Taurus

Element: Earth

Modality: Fixed

Strengths: Dependable, logical, pragmatic, sensual, stable, and trustworthy

Weaknesses: Dependent, jealous, materialistic, possessive, rigid, and stubborn

Taurus is a fixed sign, and it is also an earth sign. Because of this, it is a very grounded, down-to-earth sign. Taureans are not only practical, but they are also known for their sensual nature, their love of the finer things, and their appreciation of the material world. Taurus is also ruled by the planet Venus, and as such, pleasure and beauty are important to a Taurus. As a fixed earth sign, Taurus takes the slow but steady and scenic route. They pause to appreciate the beauty of life. Taurus is represented by the bull, and combined with the fixed modality, there is no persuading or moving a Taurus if they are not willing. Taurus is known to be a stubborn sign, but that is because they are deeply rooted in their beliefs and their general being.

Gemini

Element: Air

Modality: Mutable

Strengths: Adaptable, communicative, curious, intelligent, outgoing, and social

Weaknesses: Fickle, impulsive, nervous, nosy, superficial, and unreliable

The sign of Gemini is an air sign and a mutable one, meaning this sign has a sociable and adaptable energy. Gemini is ruled by the planet Mercury, which assists Gemini in being a very communicative sign that is focused on broadening not only their social circles but their minds as well. This is a sign that works with its connections and has an innate ability for networking. This sign is represented by twins due to the duality of its mind. The minds of Geminis process information quickly, which helps to give them an intellectual nature, but it is one that is known to bore easily. Due to this, they can come across as fickle at times.

Cancer

Element: Water

Modality: Cardinal

Strengths: Adaptable, compassionate, imaginative, intuitive, loyal, and nurturing

Weaknesses: Codependent, crabby, jealous, manipulative, moody, and oversensitive

Cancer is a sign that is ruled by the moon, and as such, it is a sign of intuition and introspection. Cancers are referred to as the "mothers of the zodiac," and they are known for their nurturing nature. Cancer is both a water sign and a cardinal sign. This cardinal energy helps them in being driven and capable of putting plans into motion. Cancer is symbolized by the crab, and this is indicative of a moody and occasionally crabby nature as the tides shift internally for this sign.

Leo

Element: Fire

Modality: Fixed

Strengths: Confident, courageous, determined, dynamic, influential, and passionate

Weaknesses: Arrogant, attention-seeking, controlling, dominating, show-offy, and stubborn

Leo is a fixed fire sign, which brings forth the passion and creativity for which this sign is known. Leos are represented by a lion, and this is a nod to the sheer determination and fierceness of the sign. Leos are also ruled by the sun, and this brings a bright and dynamic energy into the mix. Leos revel in the spotlight and have no problem leading the way. This is a sign ripe with confidence and ability. With this proclivity to shine, Leos can sometimes come off as showoffs, but they are really just being authentic to themselves.

Virgo

Element: Earth

Modality: Mutable

Strengths: Analytical, dependable, determined, devoted, meticulous, and practical

Weaknesses: Critical, cynical, nitpicky, obsessive, perfectionist, and prone to worrying

Virgo is a mutable earth sign, which makes it a practical and adaptable influence. The sign of Virgo is represented by the virgin or the maiden, and this is indicative of it being a sign of service. Virgos are ruled by Mercury, which gives them a quick mind and an air of intellect. This is a sharp sign. Virgos are also very meticulous, and they are adept at seeing the smaller details others might miss. Due to this, Virgos can come off as nitpicky at times, but they are really just attempting to perfect the fine details.

Libra

Element: Air

Modality: Cardinal

Strengths: Charming, collaborative, diplomatic, intellectual, peaceful, and romantic

Weaknesses: Gullible, indecisive, obsessive, passive, self-sacrificing, and superficial

Libra is an air sign and a cardinal sign. Thanks to this, Libras are known for their intellect and ability to get things done. Libras are ruled by Venus and have a keen eye for aesthetics. Their symbol is the scales, and they have an innate sense of justice. This sign is one of diplomacy, and Libras will attempt to make peace and find the greatest good in any situation. However, this ability to see multiple sides of a situation can make them appear as if they are indecisive when they are really just seeing the full scope of an issue.

Scorpio

Element: Water

Modality: Fixed

Strengths: Ambitious, bold, courageous, dedicated, driven, and passionate

Weaknesses: Clingy, destructive, jealous, manipulative, paranoid, and possessive

The sign of Scorpio is a fixed water sign, which gives this influence an intuitive, if not downright psychic, energy with an abundance of drive. This sign is represented by a scorpion, which denotes that although it is a water sign, it has no qualms with stinging if the situation calls for it. Scorpios are also ruled by Pluto in modern astrology or Mars in traditional astrology, and they are dedicated and ambitious, known for overcoming obstacles. With this high energy mixed with the emotional nature of water, Scorpios can be territorial when it comes to their relationships and can often be perceived as being possessive or jealous.

Sagittarius

Element: Fire

Modality: Mutable

Strengths: Honest, idealistic, independent, intellectual, spontaneous, and tenacious

Weaknesses: Fickle, impatient, impulsive, irresponsible, restless, and tactless

The sign of Sagittarius is a fire sign and a mutable sign, which makes this influence one of passion and adaptability. Sagittarius is ruled by Jupiter, which gives these individuals an intrinsic source of luck. The sign of Sagittarius is represented by the centaur, which is half man and half horse, and it is symbolic of Sagittarius's connection between worlds. This is a sign of expansion, and Sagittarians are known for their travels and worldly views. Sagittarians are also known for their upfront, honest nature but not their social niceties. Due to this, Sagittarians can sometimes come off as tactless or impulsive.

Capricorn

Element: Earth

Modality: Cardinal

Strengths: Determined, disciplined, intelligent, organized, practical, and strategic

Weaknesses: Condescending, pessimistic, restless, rigid, ruthless, and spiteful

Capricorn is a cardinal earth sign. With this, Capricorns are both stable and driven. Capricorns are ruled by Saturn, which governs authority and discipline. As such, Capricorns have an innate ability for leadership and the grit to achieve success. Capricorns are represented by the sea goat, which notes their earthly means but also their ability to tap into their watery creativity. This combination gives them the motivation and ability to think outside of the box. This need and drive for success is not without its downsides, though, as due to this, Capricorns can sometimes come off as ruthless and rigid.

Aquarius

Element: Air

Modality: Fixed

Strengths: Idealistic, independent, innovative, intellectual, visionary, and witty

Weaknesses: Aloof, detached, distracted, impersonal, peculiar, and rebellious

Aquarius is a fixed air sign, which gives this influence intellectuality as well as steadiness. Aquarians are represented by the water bearer. This is not a representation of them being a water sign but rather a catalyst of free-flowing movement from one plane to the next. Aquarians have a higher purpose. This sign is ruled by Uranus in modern astrology and Saturn in traditional. Uranus's influence speaks to hidden truths, and Aquarians are on a quest for this knowledge. While they are an intellectual sign, they can, at times, come across as detached or distracted due to their cerebral nature.

Pisces

Element: Water

Modality: Mutable

Strengths: Artistic, idealistic, imaginative, intuitive, kindhearted, and sentimental

Weaknesses: Escapist, evasive, moody, oblivious, overly emotional, and naive

The sign of Pisces is a water sign and a mutable sign, which brings forth intuitive and adaptable energy. When we think of mutable signs, we should think of signs that are adaptable and can ride the waves of life. Pisces are ruled by Neptune, and as such, they are dreamy and often lost in their own imaginations. This sign is represented by two fish swimming in opposite directions, and this is symbolic of Pisces's dance between worlds. While Pisces are imaginative and intuitive creatures, this ability to cross the bridge between worlds can sometimes come across as escapism or being oblivious to reality.

HOUSES

While the planets tell us *what* energy is expressed and the signs tell us the *how* that energy is expressed, the houses tell us the *where*. Each house represents a certain theme in our lives, telling us the places the planets and signs express their energy. In the reference chart, you will see the locations of their big six. The sun is in Cancer in the seventh house, the moon is in Virgo in the ninth house, Mercury is in Leo in the eighth house, Mars is in Cancer in the seventh house, and Venus is in Virgo in the ninth house. This chart was created using the Placidus house system.

There are several different systems of charting houses. Personally, I most often use the Placidus or whole sign system, but feel free to try out the different systems to see which paints a more accurate picture for your life. Some of the more popular house systems are Placidus, Koch, equal, and whole sign. The difference between them is how the individual houses are calculated. The entire chart is 360 degrees and consists of twelve houses, but how the houses are divided is dependent on the system we choose. For instance, in the equal and whole sign systems, each house covers one sign, or 30 degrees of the chart. This method was frequently used when charts were hand-drawn, as they are easier to compute manually. In the Placidus system, houses can vary in size and are often larger or smaller than 30 degrees.

First House

The first house represents ourselves. This is the house of identity, and as the first house, it is also the house of beginnings. Our ascendant is the beginning of our first house, and this lends its hand to its association of self-expression, personality, and appearance.

Second House

The second house represents our possessions, both material and intangible, as well as our finances. This house involves money, security, and self-worth. It is a house of the physical and material world and our relation to it.

Third House

The third house is the house of communication and learning. This house has an emphasis on the mental realm and, as such, involves thinking and the processes of our mind. Its focus on communication and lends its hand to a sense of community and our social lives as well.

Fourth House

The fourth house is the house of home. It is the representation of your foundations with themes of home, family, security, and lineage. This house is also representative of maternal energy and nurturing.

Fifth House

The fifth house is the house of creativity and self-expression. This is a house that represents playfulness, fun, and entertainment. It has an emphasis on pursuing your pleasures and hobbies and generally just having a good time.

Sixth House

The sixth house is the house of service. This house is concerned with matters of health, routine, fitness, and work. However, "work" refers more to what it takes to get by and the day-to-day tasks one must complete. This house rules our daily routines and overall well-being.

Seventh House

The seventh house is the house of relationships. These involve both partnerships as well as marriages. These are the one-on-one relationships that we develop with the people in our lives, be it business or personal. As such, this house also rules over contracts and business.

Eighth House

The eighth house is known as the house of transformation, and it rules our attitudes toward change or crisis. This house is considered taboo or mysterious and intimate. It deals with sexuality, death, rebirth, and the occult.

Ninth House

The ninth house is considered the house of spirituality and philosophy. It speaks to our religious beliefs and ideologies as well as our exploration. This exploration is twofold as it pertains to both physical travels as well as the expansion of our minds through learning.

Tenth House

The tenth house is the house of authority, discipline, and structure. This is the house that governs stability, ambition, and career advancement. There is also an emphasis on respect and reputation within this house in regard to our position in society.

Eleventh House

The eleventh house is the house of friendships and personal goals. While there is an emphasis on personal relationships, there is equally an emphasis on personal expansion through the pursuit of goals and aspirations. This is an innovative house that also fosters a sense of community.

Twelfth House

The twelfth house is the house of secrets and is known for what is unseen. The themes of this house include our subconscious, our imagination, and anything residing in the shadows. These can include our secrets, private affairs, our dreams, and anything that is hidden from plain sight.

Empty Houses

Most charts have approximately two to five empty houses, and while the explanation for that can be simple—there are only so many planets—an empty house is also thought to indicate areas of your life that you don't necessarily need to work on within this lifetime. These empty houses could represent areas of ease within our lives. It is also possible that the overall themes of the empty houses may not play a fundamental role in your lifetime. Whatever the case may be, if you do not have a planet in a particular house, it is not a cause for concern.

aspects

The next step in reading our natal charts involves examining the aspects within it. An aspect is when two or more planets create an angle to one another, and each aspect has a different meaning. The major aspects include conjunction, sextile, trine, square, and opposition. Aspects highlight the relationships between the planets and show us how the planets at particular angles from one another interact together.

There are some aspects that are considered favorable, and there are aspects that are considered challenging. One thing that is important to remember is that there are no "bad" aspects. Often times "easy" aspects aren't ideal because they create areas in our lives that flow too easily. While this sounds nice in theory, it does not create the grit needed to achieve goals, whereas a challenging aspect can do just that.

I will go over the five major aspects, and you can refer to the referenced chart for examples.

Conjunctions

Conjunctions are planets that are 0 degrees from one another, meaning they are either exactly on top of each other in your birth chart or very close. These create an intense energy under the signs.

Example: The moon in Virgo is in conjunction with Venus in Virgo.

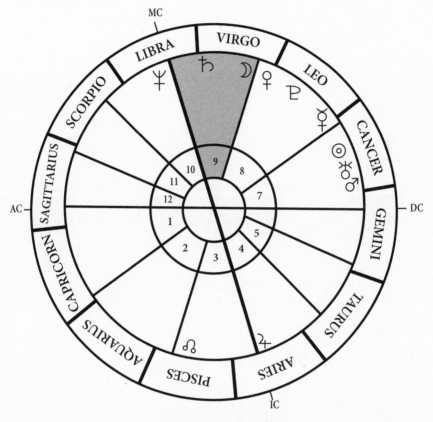

Conjunction Graph

Conjunction Symbol

Sextile

The sextile aspect is when two planets are at a 60-degree angle from each other, or roughly two signs apart from each other. This is considered a friendly aspect.

Example: The moon in Virgo is sextile to Mars in Cancer.

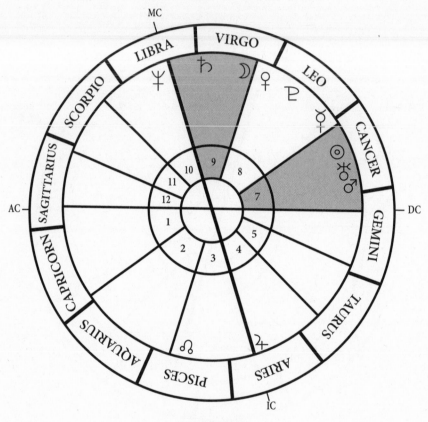

Sextile Graph

Sextile Symbol

Trine

A trine aspect is formed when planets are at a 120-degree angle from each other. These planets are roughly four signs apart from each other. This is considered a harmonious placement. It is also considered to be lucky.

Example: Jupiter in Aries is trine to Pluto in Leo.

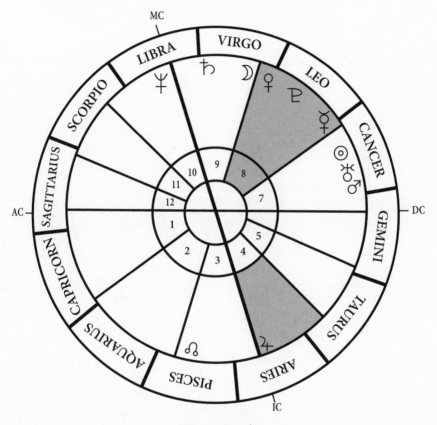

Trine Graph

Trine Symbol

Square

A square is formed when planets are at a 90-degree angle from one another. These planets are three signs apart. This is considered a hard aspect that creates tension.

Example: The sun in Cancer squares Neptune in Libra.

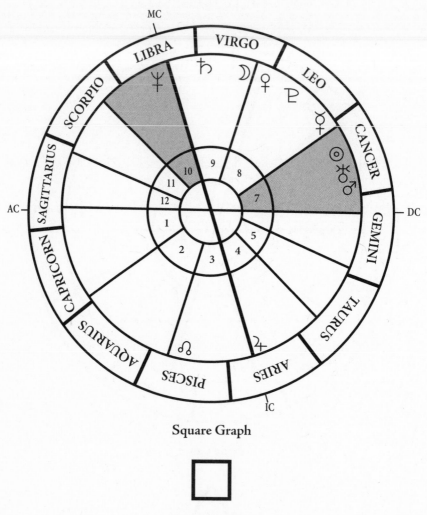

Square Graph

Square Symbol

Opposition

An opposition is when planets are directly opposite from one another on the wheel, or at a 180-degree angle from one another. This is another aspect that is considered difficult due to opposing energies being at odds with one another.

Example: Jupiter in Aries is in opposition to Neptune in Libra.

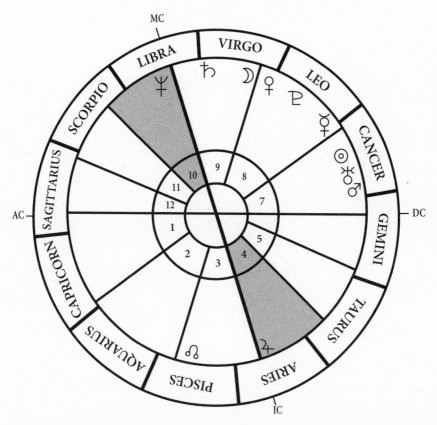

Opposition Graph

Opposition Symbol

patterns

Aspect patterns are created when three or more aspects form a particular pattern. These patterns build upon the individual aspects and create a larger picture of the driving forces behind a person. Remember, aspects themselves can show where energy flows freely and where it is met with resistance. Therefore, when these aspects form a geometrical pattern, they create an illustration of who we are and what our mission in this lifetime may be.

Each of these patterns has an individual meaning. In certain patterns, like the yod and T-square patterns, there is an "apex" planet. What this means is that there is a focal planet that becomes the most critical factor within the pattern itself.

Grand Trine

A grand trine is formed by three trines in a chart and is considered to be lucky. These combined aspects are thought to produce traits that come naturally to the individual, and this is often referred to as the "big easy."

Grand Trine

Kite

A kite is formed by a grand trine with two points sextile to another point. Typically these are considered a positive aspect as they create tension. The apex of this formation creates a focal point to the grand trine that can propel a person forward.

Kite

Grand Cross

A grand cross, also called a grand square, is formed when four planets are aligned at 90-degree angles from one another. This is a rare aspect that creates tension as it is created when four planets are separated by squares. This pattern gives dynamic energy to the planets—and the person—involved. While this is considered a hard aspect, it can produce a person with stability and perseverance. A person with this aspect may actively seek out challenges.

Grand Cross

T-Square

When two planets in an opposition square another planet, they create a T-square. This aspect provides tension and can produce a drive to succeed within a person. This is a pattern that is often found in people who are in leadership roles.

T-Square

Yod

A yod is formed by a quincunx (a lesser aspect of 150 degree) with two planets that are sextile to each other. This pattern is also referred to as "the finger of god" and is a fortunate aspect that can be indicative of a talent or a driving force in one's life.

Yod

Broom Closet Witch Tips

. . . .

Astrology is another practice that is not inherently witchy, though some religions may frown upon it. However, unless you are highly adept at hand-drawing charts, this is largely done online and through apps on our phones, which makes this practice a relatively easy thing to hide from others if you do not feel like sharing your interests. And if you do feel like connecting with others who are like-minded? There's no shortage of astrology groups on any social media platform, so you can immerse yourself with individuals who share your interests.

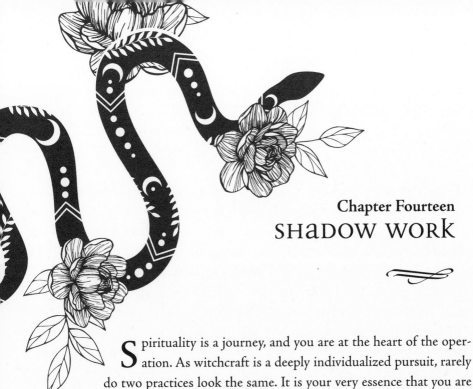

Chapter Fourteen

SHADOW WORK

Spirituality is a journey, and you are at the heart of the operation. As witchcraft is a deeply individualized pursuit, rarely do two practices look the same. It is your very essence that you are cultivating, your own energy that you are sourcing, and your own power into which you are stepping. With this comes room for personal growth, and shadow work is a great starting point. Shadow work has become a bit of a trending topic, but that does not diminish the importance of its practice.

WHAT IS OUR SHADOW?

The idea of our shadow self emerged from the works of Carl Jung, a Swiss psychologist and psychiatrist, as well as Freudian concepts of the unconscious mind. In fact, Jung's work built upon some of the Freudian concepts. Jung's work influenced much of what we know about archetypes and personalities today, and he developed the concepts of introverted and extroverted personality types as well as the collective unconscious.[66] His work maintained that our shadow selves were the parts of us that were unknown to us. These could be buried, repressed, or otherwise hidden for us to assimilate within society.

Jung was a proponent of using dream analysis to dig into our shadow selves by identifying how they present themselves in our dreams. He believed that our shadow selves often presented themselves in our dreams as the same gender as the

---

66. Fordham, Fordham, and the Editors of *Encyclopaedia Britannica*, "Carl Jung."

one we identify with.[67] Our dream shadow self could take shape in many forms. It may be presented to us as ourselves and highlight our fears, or it could appear as an antagonist and highlight an otherwise hidden element to us. And while dream analysis is an excellent way to divulge information about your psyche and highlight your shadow self, it is not the only method.

It is important to remember that our shadow self is not inherently negative. Our shadow is formed through our lifetimes, and it is a culmination of traits that we felt the need to repress or hide, and these are not always "bad" traits. Think of vulnerability. This trait is a characteristic that many people struggle with, but it is not a bad trait to possess. In fact, it shows a tremendous amount of courage to allow yourself to be vulnerable. This is probably the furthest thing from an undesirable trait, but it is one that people can be shamed into repressing. Our shadow side is formed out of necessity and survival, often early on in our lifetimes, but it expands and compounds over the course of our lives. Our shadow self can be formed out of a myriad of traits, and while it is true that some may not be considered "desirable," you can often find traits that are "desirable" buried within your subconscious.

IDENTIfYING OUR SHADOW

Jung believed that becoming conscious of your own shadow took a great deal of effort and that it consisted of acknowledging the darker aspects within yourself.[68] With this in mind, understand that identifying one's shadow is a lengthy, ongoing process. To begin, you can start to identify your shadow self by homing in on parts of your personality that you have kept hidden.

To be able to identify your shadow self requires a level of digging into yourself that could be painful for those with unresolved traumas. Before you proceed with this journey, you must check in with yourself. If you feel that you are in a proper headspace for this work, you can move forward. However, having a therapist's assistance is an invaluable part of this process—especially if you intend to poke and prod at areas that you have repressed. This can dredge up painful memories you might not be able to process without a professional. If this is at all a possibility, first set up counseling in any capacity that you can. Once this step

67. Jung, *Man and His Symbols*, 177.
68. Jung, *The Archetypes and the Collective Unconscious*, 20.

is complete, you can move toward identifying the hidden elements of your own personality.

The first step in incorporating shadow work into your practice is the process of identifying your shadow. This can be accomplished in a few ways, which I will go over here. The most important part is to stay mindful of your responses and create an honest dialogue with yourself. You needn't judge yourself. Instead, remain open and objective.

Assess Your Triggers

Consider the times when you have had an explosive or visceral reaction to an occurrence or event. When exploring this, it is important to note what the instance was, what your reaction was to it, and what could be the underlying cause of why you reacted that way. Was there a situation in your past that has made you more sensitive to this particular situation? Identifying your triggers is paramount in assessing what they are and what they are rooted in.

Assess Your Judgments

There is this fun thing that we are all guilty of called "projection." While nobody is particularly fond of admitting it, as it is much easier to cast judgment on someone else than it is to reflect upon ourselves, we have all been guilty. My personal projection? Laziness. In the past, I have mentally shredded someone a new one for perceived laziness. It was a long road to discovering that this was a variation of a trait that I once possessed but had repressed due to necessity. Instead, I overcorrected and became a tireless, ambitious shrew. To this day, I struggle with overextending myself, but I have learned not to judge those who have the ability to relax. Now I am in awe of their ability to go with the flow. With this information in mind, can you think of a character trait that you can't stand in another person? If you could sit with this trait for a moment, could you identify it as a part of yourself or once a part of yourself? Bring it to the surface.

Acknowledge Your Patterns

If you have ever watched the cult classic *Groundhog Day* (1993) starring Bill Murray, you have probably got a good understanding of the monotony that comes along with repeating the same day, or life, over and over again. If you have not, a quick synopsis is that Bill Murray's character is forced to repeat the same

February day until he undergoes a massive character transformation. While this is cinematic fiction, the same logic applies to the real world too. Until we identify our own patterns, we will carry out the same monotonous lessons until they are labeled and dealt with. These patterns can manifest in different areas of our lives, but often they come in the form of self-destructive behaviors. These behaviors could be habits or decisions we make or toxic partners we entertain. The first step in breaking a pattern is to acknowledge that the pattern exists.

Acknowledge Your Traumas

This particular step is never a pleasant one to delve into, and if you have a signif-icant amount of trauma in your life, I encourage you to seek out a counselor who can help you both dissect these issues and start the process of healing from them. However, if you feel ready, acknowledge the traumas you have endured within your lifetime. Label them, sit with them, and dig into how they have presented themselves and how they have affected the person you've become. Remember, trauma to one person is not the same as trauma to another person, and your expe-riences are not less valid if they weren't as bad as X, Y, Z. What is relevant is the emotional or physiological effects that these events had on you, your devel-opment, and your understanding of the world around you. Reflect on your own personal history and the moments that left wounds or divots within you and sit with them. While you are under no obligation to forgive the perpetrators, if there are any, you should work toward forgiving yourself. Make note of the responses you have that directly or indirectly correlate with these events and identify them.

Address Your Subconscious Thoughts

Another facet of yourself to be mindful of is your subconscious thoughts. These are your automatic thoughts. Now, while several of your thoughts may tend to be on autopilot, this refers to the voice in your head that is unkind, makes snap judgments, or deviates from the "you" that you have accepted as yourself. These subconscious thoughts can have roots in our traumas, but on their own, they can assist us in uncovering truths about ourselves and the parts of ourselves that we have repressed. Personally, my brain can be unkind to me from time to time, and I know this to be true for others as well. In an effort to reprogram, I have taken to answering these intrusive thoughts aloud with rebuttals. And while I do not recommend doing this in public—unless you have no qualms with concerned stares—this can assist in meeting these thoughts head-on. When these thoughts do occur, take a moment to dissect them. Where do these thoughts stem from? Was there an instance in your life where you were made to feel this way by others? Is this *really* how you feel? Ask yourself pertinent questions as you dive into these thoughts.

SHADOW WORK JOURNAL PROMPTS

One of my favorite methods for digging into shadow work is journaling, as that is a tangible process. You may have picked up throughout these pages that I am a big advocate for writing things down, and you would be correct. Personally, as both an introvert and a writer, there are times when I am unable to assess the full scope of how I feel about an issue until I see it literally spelled out in front of me. With this in mind, I am including several journal prompts that you can apply to your own shadow work journey.

Journaling in general is a therapeutic act, and that is no different when it comes to using journaling as a tool for processing shadow work. While the following prompts are a good start, they are not part of an all-inclusive list. In order to create a more personalized prompt, ask yourself specific "why" questions pertaining to your own life, and continue asking yourself why until you uncover a previously hidden truth. While that sounds simple, drilling down to our core with a series of "why" questions can be unbelievably transformative. Do not limit yourself to the following prompts. This is your process, so personalize it in a way that is applicable to your life and your experiences.

+ What is a trait that bothers me in other people? Does that trait exist within me?
+ What emotions do I avoid, and why do I avoid them?
+ What would be the worst way someone else could describe me? Why?
+ Do my parents' values differ from my own? How so?
+ How would I like to improve myself and why?
+ What scares me and why do I think it does?
+ Do I trust myself? Do I trust others? Why do I feel this way?
+ When reflecting on my childhood, what do I feel and why do I feel this way?

- ◆ Am I honest with myself? What do I hide from myself?
- ◆ What are my greatest strengths? What are my greatest weaknesses?
- ◆ Have I forgiven myself?
- ◆ Write a letter to someone who hurt you.
- ◆ Write an apology letter to yourself.

Rather than tackling these prompts all at once, aim to focus on them one at a time. Allow yourself the time to journal one out and sit with the thoughts and feelings that occur. Shadow work is a marathon rather than a sprint. Only in this case, there is no finish line. While you work through the thoughts these prompts bring into your consciousness, acknowledge the feelings surrounding them. Dig into the roots of the thoughts. Do you understand where these feelings are emerging from? Is there a single incident or a culmination of many? Journal out the messages you receive from yourself as well as the emotions that arise.

INTEGRATING YOUR SHADOW SELF

Once your shadow self has been identified and you have dug into the depths of its causes as well as how it presents itself, you must learn how to integrate it. This is not to say that we have to *become* our negative traits, but we must make peace with them. The purpose of integration is to offer ourselves forgiveness for being multifaceted beings with both light and dark coursing through our veins. We are never all good or all bad. We are a multitude of traits, and it is through acceptance and forgiveness that we can begin to feel whole. Also, by acknowledging our shadow self, we lessen its overall impact. Again, do not be discouraged if this is a continuous process. It is supposed to be. We are beings experiencing human existence, and this, by its very nature, is a complex and complicated endeavor.

If, through your reflections, you have realized that you have repressed a trait that you understand is positive, exercise bringing that trait into the light. Note: This will feel incredibly foreign at first. You may feel like a fish out of water or like you have shown up naked to class. This is okay. This is perfectly normal. Your shadow will resist this process with all its might because it works best in the dark corners of your mind, but continue to take baby steps into bringing it to the forefront. It does not have to be done in one fell swoop. This is not something that happens overnight.

The process of integration is not to fully embody our negative attributes, but rather, it is to shine a light on what exists within us so it loses its power. The unacknowledged shadow runs rampant when it is in the dark. This is its prime arena; it is where it is most comfortable, and it reigns supreme. By acknowledging its existence, we are diffusing its power.

I do not view integration as a one-stop shop or a one-and-done practice. Rather, I view the process of shadow work and integration as a lifelong process in self-improvement and healing. Perfection is not the goal here. The goal is to continually progress. Therefore, there is not likely to be a point when our work is "done" or when we've completed our mission. Life will continue to happen, and there will be more work to be done, and that is okay. We will need to retrace the steps of identifying our shadows and bringing them to light many times throughout our life. However, what we accomplish by shadow work is growth, and the value in that is immeasurable.

What does this all have to do with witchcraft? That depends on whom you ask. Some might say nothing at all. Some may claim that this is a New Age concept, and they may be right to an extent, as the two are not mutually exclusive. In fact, I would argue that pursuing growth and harnessing our minds is a crucial part of witchcraft. Witchcraft is bending energy to our will and in our favor, and this works best with a clear mind, acceptance, and the ability to tap into necessary energies without them being clouded. Shadow work allows us to have more control of our own minds and energy, which is a fundamental asset for any practitioner.

Broom Closet Witch Tips

The process of shadow work can go by many names, and by its nature, it is merely the process of coming to peace with ourselves in our entirety by recognizing our patterns, triggers, and hidden aspects. This is a process that does not have to be shouted from the rooftops, and it can exist solely in your mind or the safety of journals that are only for your eyes.

If a person happens to inquire about the work that you are doing on yourself, you can cite the practice as an interest in psychology or mindfulness or simply an act of growth. But you are under no obligation to explain your process to anyone. If you do not feel like discussing the matter, a simple "It is personal," should suffice to honor your own boundaries. Shadow work is a personal journey that is not meant to be shared with others, and it is a personal pursuit that can be undertaken without any tools necessary, although I highly recommend a notebook and pencil.

Furthermore, the process of shadow work assists everyone—whether they're a witch or not. If a person does discover what you are working on, your secret is still safe. You are working on becoming a better person by acknowledging your own inner workings and making peace with yourself. Who can fault a person for being on the path to self-discovery and improvement?

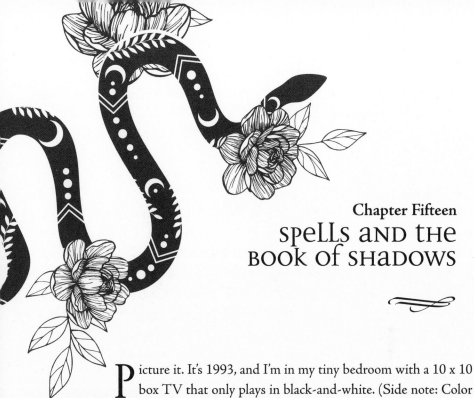

spells and the book of shadows

P icture it. It's 1993, and I'm in my tiny bedroom with a 10 x 10 box TV that only plays in black-and-white. (Side note: Color TVs existed in the '90s—but I did not have one.) The TV is connected to my state-of-the-art VHS player, and I'm watching a copy of *Hocus Pocus* (1993) rented from the local video store. I'm living the dream.

That movie was my first peek into spells and the gloriously bound books that housed those magickal enchantments in living color. Not *in* color exactly, but the books weren't animated, making them all the more real for a young child like myself. Fictional as the story may have been, I was absolutely enchanted.

Truth be told, I'm just as enchanted with books in modern times—magickal or otherwise. In this chapter, I will cover the process of writing and recording spells and what to record your spells *in*, as that is an important part of the process as well. Did you know hand cramps from extensive writing are an integral part of the craft? Don't worry—they're not. We are in the digital age, and spell books can be handwritten or stored digitally. The choice is yours. As such, I will include a discussion on the naming of these magickal books, ideas for creating your own, and suggestions for what to include in it.

book of shadows and grimoires

The term *Book of Shadows* is often used interchangeably with the term *grimoire*, and what you call your own spell book is entirely up to you. That said, there are a couple of different schools of thought on the difference between the two. One such thought is that *Book of Shadows* is exclusively a Wiccan term, whereas the term *grimoire* is not. In this perspective, they are fundamentally the same. Another thought is that a grimoire is typically a reference book that can be shared more openly, while a Book of Shadows is largely considered more private, but both are still sacred to a practitioner.

In this instance, grimoires act more as guides to performing magick, and they can sometimes be considered the textbooks of magick. These books house instructions on tools, correspondences, and different materials that a witch can utilize in their practice, whereas a Book of Shadows would be the record of a witch's personal journey. This could include their own spellwork, their natal charts, their beliefs, or even records of their dreams. This could be considered a witchy journal of sorts, and it is a living record of their personal path. While the two terms do differ, there are no rules restricting you from combining the two if you so choose.

Many times, witches use binders as their spell books as this allows them to conveniently insert pages where they are needed to keep them most cohesive. But if you are good at preplanning or are not fond of binders, you can choose from any number of beautiful notebooks or journals out there. Many of my Books of Shadows are what I would consider "organized chaos." Personally, this does not bother me, as my brain formed a connection to when and where I wrote the words and I can locate what I need quickly. No two people are exactly alike, though, so choose a format that appeals to you.

Once you have found the perfect place to record your magick, you must decide on the contents. Will it be a grimoire? Will it be a Book of Shadows? Will it be both? Once you have made your decision, you can take the time to organize. Map out how the book will flow and list the topics you want to include. If you are using a binder, you will not need a rigid guide as you'll always have the flexibility to rearrange as necessary. But if you are not, a little preplanning will go a long way in the overall flow of the book. I will provide a list of ideas to help get you started on this, but please understand that these are your sacred books. They belong to you, and there is no right or wrong way to craft and keep them.

Now that you have picked out your book and have a basic idea of what you are going to include, here comes the fun part: deciding how you want your pages to look. If you prefer a simple, clean look, basic labels and text may be all that you need, but if you like a little more pizzazz, there is so much room for creativity. I have seen beautiful Books of Shadows that are arranged much like a scrapbook of witchy content with borders, images, and other artistry. These embellishments create such an atmospheric ambiance that the pages themselves almost scream "magick." If you are an artist with the capability of drawing, you can draw images to go right along with the contents of the pages. Still, if you struggle or simply don't wish to draw, there is no shame in printing and pasting images or even using stickers to adorn the pages of your book. This book should be a reflection of you. Things to include:

+ Color correspondences
+ Common symbols
+ Crystal correspondences
+ Deities
+ Dream analysis
+ Elements
+ Grounding and centering
+ Herb correspondences
+ How to cast a circle
+ Lunar phases
+ Natal charts
+ Personal entries
+ Protection magick
+ Rune meanings
+ Spells and their results
+ Tarot meanings and spreads
+ Zodiac signs

You may notice that several of these suggestions can be found in the pages of this book, and that was intentional. I hope that this book serves as a reference as you carve out your own practice and step into your own power. These pages are filled with contents from my own grimoires or Books of Shadows, and hopefully, some of this information will find its way into yours.

WRITING YOUR OWN SPELLS

One of the driving forces in the creation of this book was for it to not be another spell book. While there is nothing wrong with spell books and using them as guides as you step into your own magick, the most important part of your practice is still you. You are the magick. When we couple our desires with the materials we have gathered intentionally and sit down to write and perform our own spells, we are harnessing our personal power.

If you are at the preliminary stages of your practice, it is perfectly acceptable to feel overwhelmed. The most important part is to know that you are not alone. We were all once starting out on this journey, but you must also know that we are all still carrying out this journey. There is no such thing as mastery—only growth. As we learn, we grow and evolve, and our practices change over time. This is not only normal but an excellent sign. We are not stagnant beings. We're witches. We are strong and adaptable. Take your time figuring out what calls to you. You do not need to overload yourself in the beginning.

Start with meditation, trance states, and feeling the energy around you. Once you can connect with energy, learn to play with it. Feel it in the palms of your hands. Practice directing it. This is a very simplified version of the topics covered at the beginning of this book, but this should be your first focus. Afterward, move on to protection magick in order to safeguard yourself when you tap into realms that you might not be adeptly familiar with. I covered this more thoroughly in chapter 2, and it was at the beginning of the book for a good reason. Make sure you have your protections in place.

Once you have had time to acclimate yourself, it is time to start writing your own spells. Yes, you can do this. You have all the tools you need inside of yourself. It is time to be a scientist of sorts. Take out your Book of Shadows. It is time to make an entry.

Step One: Set the Intention

Set your intention. What is your desire? What is it that you are hoping to accomplish by performing magick? Sit with this question until you can articulate it. Remember that it needs to be specific and clear. You want there to be no confusion as to the outcome that you desire.

Step Two: Select the Materials

Will this be a candle spell? A jar spell? A sachet? Will you utilize kitchen magick? Will you recite an incantation? Set your stage. Once you know what method you would like to use, determine the supplies that are needed. There are materials that can assist you in crafting your spellwork in the pages of this book, and you are more than welcome to start small.

Step Three: Assign Meaning

While you may be using herbs, crystals, salts, and the like, many of these materials have multiple purposes. Assign each component of your spell its specific task. Take rosemary, for example. There are several different properties associated with this plant. If I am creating a spell for self-love, it is not the property of banishing that I am after. While the intention is not everything, it is still important. Let your materials know what it is you are using them for. Write this use down in your Book of Shadows.

Step Four: Raise Energy

Raising energy can be quite simple if you do not overthink it. There are several methods included in this book. If you work with deities, you may ask to tap into their energies. If you work with the elements, you may ask them to lend theirs. However, some spellwork does just fine with the use of our own energy. Consider the size of the task. Will you need reinforcement? To raise your own energy, you can focus on taking shallow breaths until your heart rate increases and you can feel the energy building. If this method does not work for you, try movement. Once you have raised enough energy and you feel it pulsating within you, it is time.

Step Five: Perform Your Spell

Now it is time to make some magick—quite literally. Keeping your intention at the forefront of your mind, channel all the energy you have raised into the creation of your spell—into the combining of ingredients, into the lighting of the candle, or into the stirring of the pot. Allow the energy coupled with your intention to flow into the creation of the spell and outward into the universe for it manifest. Record your practice and how your spell felt in your Book of Shadows.

If you have borrowed energy from outside sources, thank the sources and return the excess.

Step Six: Rest and Recharge

It is called spell*work* for a reason. It takes a certain amount of effort and energy to direct your magick, and this is the time to unplug and recharge. Replenish your energy with nourishing foods or run yourself a bath. Take time to rest. This is a necessary step in the process. Do not run yourself dry. However, it is possible you could feel the opposite after completing your work, particularly if you are utilizing outside energies. If you are still buzzing with energy, practice grounding. This can be as simple as going outside and placing the souls of your feet in the earth, or you can direct your palms toward the ground to feed the energy away from you. Grounding can also be combined with meditation. Find the method that works for you. This takes practice, and that is okay. Different strokes for different folks.

Step Seven: Record Results

This step cannot be overlooked if we want to learn and grow from our spellwork. Did our manifestation come to be? Did it manifest in a way that we did not consider or want? Write down every necessary detail in your Book of Shadows so you can come back to it and determine what you might need to alter next time for it to be successful. This is not an exact science, but it is a lot like science in that we have to develop our hypothesis, run tests, and review the data. Admittedly, when I want to flatter myself, I refer to myself as a scientist. I rather enjoy the idea of being some disheveled witchy scientist testing out her solutions and compiling her data.

WHEN SPELLS DON'T WORK

There will be times when we perform magick and the spell either doesn't seem to work, or it appears to have "misfired" or "backfired." For instance, I once set the intention to "make double my paycheck in a single check." It manifested, all right. When I switched jobs, I was paid biweekly instead of weekly; therefore, I made double my previous in a single paycheck. That wasn't as much of a misfire as it was a mistake on my part for not being more clear and more concise with my intentions. Technically the spell *worked*. For all purposes, I got precisely what I asked for. It wasn't what I meant, but it was what I stated and what I focused on.

At times when our spells seem to have gone awry, we can take it as an opportunity to look inward. We can practice stating our intentions and desires clearly and specifically so we can attract what we're hoping to achieve.

However, there are other times when our actual desires don't mesh with what we are requesting. Perhaps we're hoping to attract a partner into our lives who is well put together and established, but we're still struggling with our own feelings of inadequacy or coming to terms with our own toxic traits. Or maybe we're after a higher paid and more prestigious job but also don't feel that we're in a place for more responsibility, and we like the small task load in our current position. During these moments, we must be honest about our actual desires in order to create clear and specific intentions. It may be best if we address the foundational circumstances before moving on to the next thing. In the case of the job, we could focus on a spell to motivate us to tackle more tasks or to free up more time so we can devote it to advancement before doing a spell to land that more prominent position. In the case of bringing in a partner, it may be best to delve deeper into our shadow work before working on attraction. These are just two examples in a sea of circumstances, and they hardly cover all the variables of human existence.

That said, there are times when our spells will not work through no fault of our own. Life is energy and constant motion. By performing our own spells, we are telling the universe what we want, but we are but one point in the vast universe. While we can sway the odds in our favor, we may not be able to stop what is already in motion.

It is also highly possible that we were unable to generate enough energy in our workings to sway the hands of fate in our favor. While we can make changes in our reality through manipulation of energy and assertion of our will, there can be operational hiccups, and a failure to raise an adequate amount of energy coupled with unclear intentions is high on the list of possibilities. In this case, we can go directly back to the drawing board. If you're not confident in your ability to work with energy, refer to the section about directing energy in chapter 1. Work with the formation of an energy ball until you can feel it tangibly. This is often described as tingling or a sensation akin to static electricity. Keep feeding energy into it either from your own reservoirs or from outside sources. Once you can feel this ball of energy, imbue it with your intention. Feel the physical change within the energy mass. Now you can take this ball of energy and channel it into your spellwork.

Whatever the reason your spellwork didn't come to fruition, the best thing you can do to advance in your practice is *to* practice. Start with the basics and work your way up. Add to your practice, little by little, as you build confidence in your own abilities and as you step into your power. This is a practice that takes time to develop, but it is wholeheartedly worth the energy that we put into it. Even the spells that do not turn out as planned or the spells that seemingly do not work are all guiding us on this journey. They are our practice. They are the lessons to build upon and learn from. We take from these lessons an acquired knowledge that helps us navigate through our journey onward through this winding path.

Broom Closet Witch Tips

Keeping spell books, grimoires, and Books of Shadows can be a little harder to hide without some level of privacy, but the digital world does offer us some level of anonymity or, at the very least, the ability to not have physical copies lying around. Despite not being in the broom closet, I have both a physical grimoire and a digital grimoire. I keep the physical copy because I find there is magick to the written word, and I keep the digital copy because the search feature and its portability are unmatched.

The benefits of living in the digital age can be applied to occult books as well. While I urge you to practice your magick, there is no harm in reading books that pique your interest, and you can use e-books to make sure your physical copies are not found. There are also several sites that allow you to access full libraries of certain occult books for a small monthly fee. Also, many public libraries offer a similar service as well, and all that's needed is a library card.

However, if you love the magick that physical books offer, there are ways to make them inconspicuous as well. You can invest in book covers or make your own so you can read them without raising any eyebrows or keep them on the shelves. And if they are found? You can always use the excuse that you are working on a school project or that you are writing a book.

everyday magick

t he purpose of everyday magick is to place an emphasis on our ordinary, everyday tasks and transform them into a part of our spiritual practice. This process helps us in several ways, such as boosting our confidence in our abilities, helping us remain mindful, and keeping us in tune with our spirituality. In chapter 5, I discussed one of my favorite methods of everyday magick: enchanting my drinking water. If it sounded incredibly simple, that is because it is. And really, that is the beauty of creating your own practice.

This chapter will include simple methods that you can incorporate into your practice from your everyday life, allowing you to connect with your power on a daily basis. The purpose of this is to bring magick into the mundane. And this process gives me life. The more we connect to our magick and the more we allow ourselves to practice, the more we advance our ability. That is not to say you will never find yourself in a rut. No, that is not the case, as life tends to happen at several "WTFs" per hour. But we can build upon our everyday habits in a way that allows us to also develop ourselves on a spiritual level while living out our daily grind.

glamour magick

Glamour magick, which is a topic of frequent interest, is a method that allows you to access your magick on a regular basis. If you have watched the 1996 cult classic film *The Craft*, you may remember the scene where the main characters have a sleepover and Sarah changes her eye color from green to brown. Then, when asked to do something "bigger," she changes her hair color from brown to a shade of blonde. While those transformations may not be within your reach without colored contacts and a trip to the salon, what the character was demonstrating were acts of glamour magick.

Glamour magick influences our appearance and our outward persona largely through the use of enchantment, mantras, and color magick. We intentionally select items that correspond with characteristics we want to embody and enchant items that we use daily, such as our makeup, clothing, perfumes, or brushes. Many times, a person finds that they have been incorporating glamour magick in their daily practice without even being aware of it. And while that is an amazing act of intuition, we can level this up with a more focused intention.

In glamour magick, you can imbue your makeup brushes with intentions, such as confidence, allure, mystery, beauty, attraction, or any other attribute you wish to embody. You can also do this with your jewelry, clothing, compacts, eyeshadows, blushes, lipsticks, or any other makeup and beauty items.

While those methods are great ways to enhance your confidence, you can also use glamour magick as a form of protection. This can be done in several different ways, including imbuing your jewelry with the task of protection or enchanting your makeup as a layer of protection against harm.

But there is another option as well; you can make use of color magick. When selecting your outfit for the day, make use of color associations to choose what you would like to personify that day. The act of being intentional will further assist you in showing up that day as whatever it is you hope to achieve. For protection, you can choose clothing in black, blue, or brown to channel the color's protective properties. If you need confidence or need to channel strength, you could wear colors like orange or red. Refer back to the list of color associations in chapter 11 for more ideas.

Glamour Magick Ideas

- ✦ Carry rose quartz and rhodochrosite for attraction
- ✦ Draw beauty sigils on mirrors
- ✦ Draw sigils with makeup
- ✦ Enchant jewelry

+ Enchant makeup brushes
+ Enchant your outfit
+ Imbue perfume with confidence
+ Use color magick for outfits
+ Use makeup for protection

Enchanting Items

Enchanting an item, such as our makeup or our water, is the act of imbuing an object with a specific intention energetically. If you want to incorporate lunar cycles into this practice, remember that the New Moon is the time of setting intentions, which makes it a great time for enchanting items.

The first step in enchanting an item is to build up energy. This can be done by concentrating on building your own energy or by pulling energy from outside sources. It can also be accomplished through motion, such as dance or physical activity. Once you have built enough energy (and you will know because you will feel as if you're ready to burst at the seams in order to release it) you must hold the item you wish to enchant or place it nearby. This largely depends on the size of the object and whether it's physically possible to hold it within your hand.

Next, place the intention at the forefront of your mind. This can be done by repeating the phrase or trait you want to imbue the object with, by visualizing how the trait feels, or by combining a mixture of the two. The method or methods you pick depends on what feels right for you and allows you greater focus.

Once the intention is set in your mind's eye, place your hands on the object, and focus on transferring the energy that has built up within you into the object itself. The energy within you should start to dial down, and you should be able to feel the energy around the object now. Wave your hand around the object. The energy should be palpable. You should feel tingles or spikes of energy in your fingertips and palms. This is how you know the intention has been transferred to the object.

Witchcraft in Action
enchanting your makeup

It's time to enchant our makeup and put glamour magick into action. For this exercise, we'll focus on confidence and use a single article of makeup. This can be your foundation, eyeshadow, perfume, or any other personal item that suits your needs.

Before enchanting an item, I like to remove any lingering energies surrounding them by the use of smoke cleansing, and the following exercise includes these steps.

Materials:
* * Item of makeup or perfume
* * Herb bundle or incense
* * Lighter or matches

Directions:
1. Remove any lingering energies surrounding the item you wish to enchant by lighting the herb bundle or incense. Take the item in your hand and waft the smoke toward it.
2. After the item has been cleansed, focus on building up your own positive energy.
3. Keep your sights on raising positive energy; let it build as you keep your intention of confidence in mind. Once you feel as if the level of energy is ready to burst, place the item in your hand.
4. Focus on channeling all the energy you've built up—along with the intention of confidence—directly into the item.
5. Once you feel your energy take root in the item, it's ready for use. It can be your armor in tackling the days ahead.

fitness magick

In my opinion, this type of magick doesn't get enough airtime. Fitness magick can be considered an extension of glamour magick as you can utilize many of the same practices, but it has other uses as well. Remember in the previous section where I mentioned that a way to raise energy is physical motion? What better way to combine raising energy for spellwork than to drum it up while bettering our general health. Formal exercise might not be as fun as dancing naked under the moon, but it can be. In fact, dancing is an excellent way to raise energy, sans clothes or otherwise. When we exercise, we dial into an energy that can be utilized in our magick, and we can transfer this energy directly into our intentions. Many of these same concepts are used in sex magick, though that is not a topic for this book. Maybe the next one.

This building of energy works best in higher intensity workouts, such as cardio or high-intensity interval training (HIIT), where we are building momentum. That is not to say that lower-intensity workouts do not have their place in fitness magick. They do, but for the purpose of building energy, let us concentrate on exercises that get our heart rate up.

To practice fitness magick, you must set an intention in your mind. For an alternative method, you can draw sigils on your body with lotion or onto your thermos with a marker or by tracing your finger alongside it and channel power into the sigils as you work out. If sigils are not your thing, simply focus on your intention. Now get active. As your heart rate and energy increase, direct the energy into the intention to power it before releasing it outward into the universe.

Fitness magick is not limited to cardio, though. Fitness magick can even be performed through practices such as yoga as you use this time as means to channel your energy. You can also combine nature and fitness magic by taking a stroll through the woods, a park, or wherever you feel most comfortable. Safety first. The purpose of combining magick and the mundane is to be mindful of your actions and to combine the physical with the spiritual. Take in the world around you as you take this stroll. Feel the wind, feel the sun, and observe the growth around you. Ground yourself and tap into nature. If possible, take your shoes off to foster a direct connection between your skin and the earth. Be intentional and fully present.

Another way to combine your fitness regimen with your magickal life is to create spells for health, vitality, and motivation. These can be accomplished in several different ways, and in my practice I use both candle spells and jar spells to give me a cosmic kick in the ass when I've been sedentary for too long. When collecting my materials, I choose colors, herbs, and crystals that correspond with vitality, willpower, motivation, and strength. These materials can be personalized to your exact needs by choosing what aligns with your intentions.

Fitness Magick Ideas

- ✦ Channel energy through meditation
- ✦ Create a health altar
- ✦ Draw a sigil on your body or water bottle
- ✦ Enchant your water bottle
- ✦ Select gym wear for empowerment
- ✦ Utilize your energy for a purpose

Witchcraft in Action
fitness candle spell

This spell helps put things into motion when we aren't prioritizing our health in the ways that we should. This spell removes the blockages that inhibit us from accessing our motivation by calling forth health, confidence, vitality, and strength.

For this spell, I prefer to use chime or birthday candles for their quicker burn time, but you can use what you have on hand.

Materials:

- * Inscription tool, such as a thumbtack or toothpick
- * Orange chime candle (for health and confidence)
- * Red chime candle (for vitality and motivation)
- * Firesafe surface
- * Lighter or matches

Directions:

1. Using your inscription tool of choice, inscribe your orange candle with the Uruz rune symbol for strength and inscribe your red candle with Ansuz for inspiration. Both of these symbols can be found in chapter 11. Remember that you can write words that align with your intentions as well.

2. Place each candle on the firesafe surface.

3. Light each candle. As they burn, focus first on releasing the blockages that prevent you from tapping into your motivation. You can take your hand and pull the energy blockages away from your body. Wave the energy free by shaking your hands away from you.

4. As the candles continue to burn, shift your focus to tapping into your motivation and vitality. They have been present, only hidden. Focus on bringing them to the surface.

5. Once your candles have burned down, the spell is complete. Alternatively, if you are using larger candles, you can snuff out the flames and repeat this process as needed.

KITCHEN WITCH

We have touched on kitchen witchery throughout this book, but there is perhaps no better way to create a daily connection to your practice than to make use of kitchen witchery. Sustenance is a requirement for survival, and making meals is an act of magick in and of itself. Practicing magick in the kitchen can be quite simple. All that it requires is to be intentional with your ingredients and their applications and your actions. We have a daily opportunity to infuse our meals with intentions.

In chapter 9, I discussed McCormick herbs and their correspondences. The good news is these store-bought herbs are food grade, which is an important factor when sourcing herbs for consumption. As such, this list is easy to combine with whipping up some magick in the kitchen. But kitchen witchery is not limited to the ingredients you use in a recipe. You can bring sigil witchery into the kitchen, and sigils can be drawn when you add oils to your meal or condiments to your sandwich. You can also make use of the direction in which you stir your ingredients by stirring clockwise to set intentions and counterclockwise to banish. This works with teas and coffees as well, and it can be a simple way to start your mornings intentionally. It is also a great idea to record your recipes. These notes, combined with the intentions of the meal, can make up a recipe grimoire or Book of Shadows that you can reference.

Outside of making meals, your kitchen itself can become a sacred place. As a sacred place, it should be kept tidy and be cleansed regularly. If it calls to you, you can create a kitchen altar that includes your favorite ingredients as well as your tools for making meals. If the space is large enough, you can also add fresh-cut flowers, photos, candles, or whatever you feel belongs in the sacred space. The magick of creating a dedicated place can also be extended to decorating or painting, allowing you to make use of color magick in your selections. My own kitchen is shades of blues and reds to promote not only peace and harmony but energy and willpower as well. Creating a sacred space in your kitchen will allow you a place to practice and connect with your magick every day.

Kitchen Witchery Ideas

+ Be intentional with herbs
+ Bless your kitchen and common kitchen items
+ Create a kitchen altar
+ Draw sigils with condiments
+ Keep a recipe Book of Shadows
+ Stir clockwise to set intentions and counterclockwise to banish
+ Use color magick for painting and decorating

Witchcraft in Action
Happy Home Simmer Pot

Simmer pots are a great way to refresh your home both practically and magickally. For starters, simmer pots smell amazing, and they're at times referred to as stove-top potpourri for this reason. However, we are witches. When we add our ingredients, it is done with intention, and the intention of this simmer pot is happiness. If you need to free up space on your stove, you can use a slow cooker set on low for this as well.

Materials:

* 6 cups of water
* Medium saucepan
* Knife
* Whole orange (for happiness)

* 2 tablespoons whole cloves (for love)
* 3 to 4 cinnamon sticks (for success)
* 1 or 2 fresh rosemary sprigs (for strength and protection)

Directions:

1. Bring the six cups of water to a boil in the medium-sized saucepan.

2. Slice your orange into approximately five or six round slices, and place the slices in the pot, reciting that they are to bring happiness into your life and into your home.

3. Add the cloves to the pot and recite that they are to bring forth love for yourself and those within your home.

4. Place the cinnamon sticks in the pot and recite that they are there to foster success.

5. Place the rosemary sprigs in your pot and recite that they are there to bring strength and protection.

6. Reduce the water to a simmer. Remember to check on your simmer pot and add additional water as the water evaporates. By adding water, we can extend the life of our simmer pot for a day or two.

Daily Intentions

Setting intentions is a phrase used widely in the spiritual and occult communities, but it often is not defined with much clarity, if at all. It has even been used in the pages of this book. Most people are able to develop their own associations with the term, though they may not be able to define it outright. If you have been in either community for any length of time, you have likely heard the statement that "intention is everything," and while it's a crucial part of the process, it isn't necessarily *everything*. Often intentions are conflated with the human will or wishes, and while they may share similar elements, they are not the same.

Wishes do require thought and a certain amount of energy, but they lack the action it takes to set and release an intention. A wish is a more like idle kin to intention. While they share similar roots, they are not synonymous. Will, on the other hand, is the driving force of intention. Will is a decisive action, much like intention, and it enables us to assert our intentions into the universe for them to manifest. These two concepts work hand in hand. In short, intentions are clear and specific desires that we set verbally or visually before releasing them into the universe by our will to manifest.

When setting intentions, being specific is an absolute must. Personally, I have had many misfires when it comes to setting an intention that was too vague. Take my experience of asking to double my paycheck and being paid biweekly instead, for example. When we are setting out intentions, we must be as specific as possible. These intentions can be set as a phrase, a word, or a visual symbol as long as they represent our desires with clarity. You want to leave as little room for error as possible.

Setting intentions daily can be a way to connect with our practices more regularly. These intentions will not require the same level of effort as the intentions set for more elaborate rituals, and often they can be accomplished through our own willpower. However, the act of setting an intention for the day allows us an opportunity to be mindful, and it connects us directly with our ability to manifest. Magick requires real-life action. You can set an intention to find a job, but it is less likely to happen if you are not actively submitting your resume. Use setting daily intentions as a way to connect with your abilities on both a practical and a magickal level.

Broom Closet Witch Tips

Everyday magick is simple and very easy to practice in secrecy! Color magick, glamour magick, kitchen witchery, and the like are uncomplicated methods that you can use to connect with your practice daily. They do not require anything elaborate on your part. They simply require that you be mindful and use your intentions.

We touched on kitchen altars in the "Broom Closet" section of chapter 9, and the methods listed in this chapter are also easy to apply when you're not sharing your practice with others. The same can be said for glamour magick. Nobody must know that you're using your cosmetic products intentionally to embody certain traits. Ideally, you'll be able to use the bathroom in privacy, so draw sigils on your face with your makeup before blending or enchant your favorite perfume or cologne and spray it on before leaving the house.

Our own wardrobes may also house colors with correspondences we'd like to embody, and we need not share the reasons we chose to wear red, pink, black, or purple today. The reasons and intentions behind our selections are for our own knowledge, and we're under no obligation to disclose our personal choices. And as for fitness magick? We're just working on maintaining our physical fitness, good health, and firm glutes.

witch types

Despite what you may see clogging up your Instagram or while you are scrolling through TikTok, what makes a witch is not long dark nails, septum piercings, and dark aesthetics. While there is nothing wrong with those things, and they are wonderful in their own right, they are not necessary components to being a witch. You do not have to void your closet of color in order to be a serious witch any more than you have to justify your practice to another practitioner.

There is a wealth of information out there, and while some of it is correct, a lot of what goes viral is not law or as righteous as some may claim. One must always vet creators before trusting their word as utmost sanctity and place their own inner knowing ahead of this. Be wary of those who don't leave room for nuance or believe there is only one right way. The top practitioners on your Witch-Tok may be very knowledgeable in their own practice, but they are certainly not the be-all and end-all. And they should not be on your path to knowledge either.

There are many different traditions of witchcraft, and they all differ from the other. My own path is an eclectic path, and by that I mean that I take what I enjoy and what works for my practice and make it my own. With that said, one must be mindful of appropriation and closed practices, which I will expand on shortly. Through practice, I have personalized my own brand of magick, and much of what I share can be considered to be a UPG, or an unverified personal gnosis. What this means is that my own meditations—my own practice—have shown me what I needed to know. However, this does not invalidate my knowledge, and it will not invalidate yours.

You will get the most out of your practice when you start to create your own spells, when you bond with your tools, even if they are only your mind and limbs, and when you learn to harness and project your own energy. Your UPG is—or will be—as valid to your practice as mine is to my own. This is a talent that takes time and practice to develop. When you are starting out, your spells may fail, or they may not land exactly how you intended.

I had more misses than hits when I first started out, and even to this day, when I am not careful with my energy, I can assert it in ways that I do not intend to. Recently I wished for a person who has been foul to me—in every respect—to get caught in the act. I was seething with anger, and though I meant it, it was done carelessly and without thought. While it ended up happening, the situation unfolded in front of a person who was innocent in the scenario and hurt by the repercussions of another's actions. The trickle-down effect was anything but what I was hoping for. In my case, this could be considered a nod to being "careful what you wish for," but as a practitioner, I know the power of building and projecting my own energy. I should have known better.

While the previous passage was purposefully vague to protect the people involved, I wanted to highlight the power our emotions and thoughts have to influence the future and the potential for misfires. We are energy. Everything is energy. Witchcraft is the practice of working with that energy, drawing energy in from outside forces as well as tapping into your own, and sending that energy out to call forth what you desire.

You do not need a chest full of tools to practice magick. All you need is yourself, confidence in your own power, and some working knowledge of how to channel that power. Spell jars, candle magick, rituals, and ceremonies are great, but at the root of it all, you are manipulating energy to bend to your favor. *You*. You are your own magick, and you are all you need to practice witchcraft.

What makes a witch? That definition varies among practitioners. Some will claim the light and love witches are not witches at all because they do not sit with the intricacies of the light, dark, and shades of gray. This is but one example of the controversies you may find when participating in (or lurking around) witchcraft communities. While I agree with acknowledging the full spectrum of nature, if light and love works for someone's practice, who am I to judge? Better yet, who are the loudest voices on the internet to judge? Let them worry about themselves and their own practices, and you worry about yours.

What truly makes a person a witch is that they believe themselves to be a witch and that they practice some form of witchcraft. What type of witchcraft that is is irrelevant. As long as you identify as a witch and are in the process of carving out your own path or are already established—well, my friend—you're a witch. Welcome! I did not bake any cookies, but I can probably spare a few sprigs of rosemary for this very special occasion.

types of practices

In this section, I will cover some of the approaches and types of practices that you may come across in your research. As you begin to dig into types of practices and traditions, you will undoubtedly read or hear terms such a *solitary* or *coven* as well as *open practice* and *closed practice*. I will use this space to discuss those in a little more depth.

It is important to note that cultural appropriation and colonization can be prevalent in witchcraft, and one must be mindful of these. I, myself, have been guilty of adopting practices that I was unaware were encroaching upon another's spiritual practice. For me, this was my previous use of white sage. It wasn't until I was reprimanded for it that I began to dig further and realize the reasonings. When we are confronted with our actions being harmful to another, it can be a natural response to become defensive, but this is not where you will find true growth. We must evaluate our responses and mindsets as well as where we have acquired our information from. But most importantly, we must listen to the voices of those within the communities.

Solitary Witch

The Solitary Witch isn't a member of a coven and practices independent from a group. They did not pass an initiation outside of their own trials and tribulations, and there is likely not a high priestess to be found—unless they've assigned themselves to be one. However, just because they are a solitary practitioner doesn't mean that they won't participate in rituals or gatherings with other witches.

Coven Witch

A Coven Witch is the opposite of a Solitary Witch in that they share their practice in a group setting of like-minded individuals. Typically, there will be a high priest or priestess, who is the leader of the coven. These individuals have dedicated themselves to their practice through training and initiations. Due to this, covens are an excellent way to expand one's knowledge with the assistance of a mentor. While some traditions require a set number of members, many do not. Therefore, the size of a coven can vary from group to group.

Hereditary Witch

A Hereditary Witch is not the first of their line. Their magick comes from working knowledge passed down from their ancestors, and it is typically unique to the family and their traditions. It is likely their practice will be centered upon the teachings of their ancestors as well as honoring them.

Closed Practice

A closed practice requires its members to be initiated into or born into the practice. This is not a practice that is open to the general public. A closed practice is generally passed down through families or mentors within the specific tradition. Often there are cultural beliefs and practices that would not be understood by someone outside of the practice, and as such, it is closed to those who are not a part of the culture.

Open Practice

Open practices are open to anyone to participate in, and it is the opposite of a closed practice. In this type of practice, there are no initiations.

WITCH types

For the spirit of fun, I thought I would include a witch type synopsis in this chapter *if* I fully disclosed the fact that I am not a witch type subscriber outside of my comfortable umbrella of eclectic, which just so happens to be an unusual way of saying I do what I want. When drilling down on the labels, I tend to find the boxes to be too limiting to be applicable to my own practice, but I am not the person designing your practice. You are in the driver's seat. If modern-day witch types are your jam or you just happen to like to keep tabs on the evolutions of modern witchery, keep reading.

Crystal Witch

A Crystal Witch is, simply put, a witch who works with crystals. A practitioner who might identify with this label works with crystals in a multitude of ways, from manifesting to meditating. They connect with these slivers of earth on a profound level and utilize them to their fullest extent with proper maintenance, charging, and programming. If a need arises, they have a crystal for that.

A Crystal Witch will incorporate crystals into their practice for their healing properties, and they will use crystals in their spellwork or even to infuse their water. A Crystal Witch may even choose to explore a degree in geology. If this is not of interest to them, they are likely to ramp up their studies independently. These witches will have a proclivity for identifying gems for both their metaphysical and their material properties.

Cosmic Witch

A Cosmic Witch is a witch who works with astrology and astronomy. They know their lunar phases, the constellations, the zodiac, and their natal chart—and likely their closest friends', relatives', and that cute barista at the coffee shop's natal charts as well. They are aware of both the subtle and overt energies the cosmos provide, and they utilize this knowledge in their practice.

A Cosmic Witch harnesses these energies in their workings by timing not only their spellwork but also their decisions. Some transits bode better for business, and if you can capitalize on a cosmic boost, well, why not? Some phases of the moon are better for practicing certain types of magick than others, too, and these witches know the when and where of performing magick alongside them.

Green Witch

Green Witches are deeply in tune with nature and place a strong emphasis on the natural world in their practice. These practitioners often prefer to maintain a natural, eco-friendly lifestyle. They make use of herbs and work off the land. Gardening is likely to be a deeply personal part of their practice as well as following and celebrating the cycles of nature. This could be done alongside the sabbats or something more personalized to their geographical location.

A Green Witch pursues a nature-based practice with an interest in healing and a connection with the earth. While most witches have a connection with the earth, it is more pronounced in a Green Witch as their practice is centered on cultivating this relationship. They make use of the resources provided by nature and honor the earth with the utmost respect. These witches can be environmentalists and often participate in activism that aligns with their deep respect for nature.

Hedge Witch

Hedge Witch and *Green Witch* are terms that often get used interchangeably due to their emphasis on working with natural elements. A Hedge Witch can work with herbalism and healing as well, but they also can have an emphasis on liminal spaces and otherworldly experiences, such as astral travel. The term *flying the hedge*, which is thought to mean the space between worlds, refers to this particular witch type. As such, while their practice involves working with plants, this often goes hand in hand with astral travel.

These witches typically work in close contact with the spirits of the plants and natural items they use, and they can often be solitary practitioners. That said, the actual definition of *hedge witchery* and what it consists of varies from practitioner to practitioner. Some use the term to identify as a hedge rider, exploring liminal spaces, whereas others use it to mean an earth-based practice.

Kitchen Witch

These witches practice their magick right in the heart of their home. That's right—the kitchen, the place where meals are made with specific intentions and magick is mixed with the mundane. We all need sustenance to survive, and these practitioners marry that need with magick by making use of ingredient correspondences, crafting meals laced with magick. Food and beverages are central to their practice, and the kitchen is a sacred space.

However, this magick is not limited to the kitchen as it covers an array of practices that can be done inside the home. Think of using floor washes, making oils, drying herbs, and other homemaking undertakings. This type of witch infuses daily tasks with their practice in a way that is nurturing as well as magickal.

Eclectic Witch

This term denotes a witch that picks and chooses what they adopt in their own practice. This creates a very colorful collage of practices, all piecemealed together to create a practice that suits the individual practitioner. These witches prefer to learn about several walks of life as it pertains to witchcraft and the universe at large.

This term houses the other terminologies as well as an eclectic witch has no standardized practice to outsiders, though it feels right to them. That said, if this is your path, please be mindful of closed practices and appropriation when deciding what you would like your own practice to look like.

ADVANCING IN WITCHCRAFT

The term *baby witch* has been floating around the internet, and it is used freely to describe a new practitioner. If this title sits well with you, feel free to use it, but it does not have to be assigned to you. Some practitioners argue that there is nothing infantile about starting out on your path, even if you are a beginner. It is true that you were inspired to seek out witchcraft, and you made a conscious decision to explore this path. The term *baby* can be a misnomer, sure, and some believe it takes away from the power of whom you are becoming. However, if this is a title that resonates with you, don't let anyone dissuade you. This is your path. Titles aside, in your beginning stages, you are laying the groundwork for your abilities to come, and in this section I will expand on how to gauge whether you are advancing in your practice.

When Do I Become an Intermediate or Advanced Witch?

When do you get to step out of the confines of "baby witch" or novice? There are no set answers unless you are following a tradition where you are training under another practitioner, such as a high priestess or priest, and there are initiations in the advancement of levels. This leaves a lot of solitary practitioners scratching their heads as to when it is appropriate to deviate from the self-appointed title of beginner into more advanced levels. However, there is a twofold assessment you can use for determining your aptitude within your own practice.

If you found yourself skipping the most basic explanations within this book or sighing at the fact that you found these explanations in yet another witchcraft 101 book, congratulations! You are advancing and no longer need the play-by-play on the introductory concepts of witchcraft. The other side of this coin is found within your actual practice. While research is an important part of your endeavor, you must practice developing your skills, and this requires documentation of the results. Flip through your own Book of Shadows, and study the results that you have achieved through your application of magick. Has there been progress? If you have been making progress, congratulations yet again. You are advancing.

I steer clear of the term *mastery* almost as much as I steer clear of anyone proclaiming themselves to *be* a master, as there is always more to learn. Often self-appointed masters are little more than charlatans looking to swindle you out of your pocketbook. This is not a concept exclusive to witchcraft. This is a concept that is applicable to many walks of life. If you have read this book cover to cover, you may have noticed several points that were briefly touched on, and while I know the bare bones of the material, I am aware that there are individuals who could expand on the topic in a way that is much more eloquent and informative than my amateur grasps. These topics were included solely to pique your interest, and I invite you to research them in-depth if they've done so. This book was not designed to create your path for you but to help you expand your own practice or to introduce you to new ideas.

With this, keep in mind that you may be an expert in certain sects of witchcraft and a novice in others. This is not only perfectly acceptable but normal as well. You will always be more experienced in one arena than another. As long as you're gauging your personal growth in your recordings and you're learning, you are progressing. If you are advanced in one subject and a beginner in the next, you can still drop the novice label and refer to yourself as a seasoned witch. You will never know *everything*, and that is a good thing. This not only allows you to carve out a practice that's unique to you but sets you up for future growth. Your practice can and will evolve over time. These are positives as they are indicators of development and prevent stagnation.

While I cannot take credit for this analogy, it was something I heard in passing that I found useful, so I will share it here. I will paraphrase, of course. The comparison was one of a practitioner to a chef. The reference likened the initial stages to those of a beginner who needed to learn the proper procedures of cooking before advancing. These are the novices learning the foundations before advancement. Once these procedures were down pat, they would advance to a cook who could follow written recipes, adding substitutions as needed with more success. These are the intermediaries who have the foundational concepts under their belt, and they are building on their acquired knowledge. Once this step has been mastered, they evolve into a chef. The chef would be the final step, as they are able to not only perform all the prior steps, but they're also able to create new recipes of their own successfully. While this comparison is not exactly the gold standard, it is a way to assess where you feel you are in your own practice.

Witchcraft is both a practice and a journey. It is a winding path with no set doctrine to follow. This makes for scenic routes where you explore several different facets of practice, and it accounts for plenty of trial and error.

You will learn to navigate this world of witchcraft through your own interests, whims, and pursuits. I encourage you to follow your intuition when deciding what is right for yourself because the end result will be your very own path. This path will be one that is unique to you and that cannot be compared to the practice of another. What is theirs, is theirs, and what is yours, is yours. As you build upon your knowledge and practice year after year, you will not only learn about the world around you, but you will see spaces through new lenses and learn about yourself.

Broom Closet Witch Tips

Discovering what type of witch you identify as and what your practice will look like is a deeply personal pursuit. If you're looking to reduce your visibility, keep your journals and notebooks under lock and key. These can be hidden under your mattress, in drawers, or in the confines of password-protected apps—the latter of those being the most effective as there is nothing to physically discover.

Many creators have crafted quizzes on the internet to help you get a feel for what the overarching theme of your practice might be. While these can be fun to participate in, they do not provide definitive answers. Always take these with a grain of salt and trust yourself first and foremost.

As for whether or not you are advancing, you can gauge this in the same fashion as detailed in the main section. Making these discoveries about ourselves is an internal process. As such, they needn't be discussed with others unless we choose to do so.

CONCLUSION

When writing this book, I wanted to create a place where people could come to find out more than I can fit into the character limits (and attention spans) of a standard social media post. I wanted to house a large part of my practice in a neat package for them to bring into their own lives. I wanted readers to pick from the pages what they were going to use and to discard the rest. Cherry-picking is frowned upon in many instances, but in the case of building your own practice, it is encouraged. You do not need a leader. You are the leader. Oftentimes witchcraft is a solitary practice, and we're the masters of our own domain. This gives us a lot of creative freedom as well as the ability to express ourselves and cultivate our practices in ways that feel best to our souls. To me, this is the essence of finding our own spirituality at a core level. Through our passions and following the pursuits that make us feel alive, we can improve upon ourselves. Once we have reached an understanding of energy and vibration, we can connect with the larger collective.

Oftentimes you will hear people ask where the more advanced witch books are. This is a reasonable question with so many "101" books on the market, but there are a handful of reasons for a lack of 102 books. One reason, which I have mentioned more than once throughout these pages, is that there are varying practices. These "101" books are often glimpses into the personal practices of the authors themselves and their own experiences with the craft. From the pages of these books, you experience the craft through their unique lens. This does not have to be your lens, but hopefully, you are able to pick up a gem or two from many of the "101s" on the market.

The second reason for this is that magick, at its core, is quite simple. While there are plenty of elaborate rituals, magick is available to us all if we seek it. The methods may seem complicated, but they are quite simple. What complicates the process for most of us is self-doubt. We must first change our mindset to that of the capable and powerful entity that we are. Once we do, the rest will follow. After a practitioner has consumed a handful of these beginner books, they will often start to apply the preliminary concepts to their journey. They start to carve out their own path, and that path is going to look different from another practitioner's. It's supposed to. This is your path to walk, and your journey to take.

Quite simply, you are the captain of this ship. You are the creator of your own magick in the same right that another person is the creator of theirs. Often the advanced books we are seeking are found in the hands of individual practitioners who have tested their methods time and time again and composed their own grimoires and Books of Shadows ripe with information. But it is theirs, and it is specific to them. The nuances of their practices will differ from the nuances of yours. Their rituals, their practices, their spells, and the personal gnosis will be unique to them. It is your job to practice, record, and grow on your own path—and the best way to do this is to get your hands dirty. I would say figuratively, but sometimes it is quite literal as well.

Our own personal advancement is heavily dependent on the time we spend actively practicing. It is the process of doing that triggers growth. It is the time spent making mistakes that we make discoveries and unlock advancements we did not think were possible. But I am telling you, they are possible. Start simple and keep building. Start to compile your own notes and your own recipes. Record their components as well as the ritual and, most importantly, the results. This process will give you valuable insight into what is working for you versus what is not. Once you have this data, try again. Through this consistent state of practice, you will find what works for you in your own practice, and you will build your very own brand of magick. This development should be the ultimate goal in your practice—learn, grow, evolve, and adapt. This book is in your hands only as a launching point or a reference guide.

Blessed be.

recommended reading

intuition & psychic development
+ *Psychic Witch* by Mat Auryn
+ *Intuitive Witchcraft* by Astrea Taylor

protection magick
+ *The Witch's Shield* by Christopher Penczak
+ *Protection and Reversal Magick* by Jason Miller
+ *Of Blood and Bones* by Kate Freuler

wheel of the year
+ *Witch's Wheel of the Year* by Jason Mankey
+ *Sabbats: A Witch's Approach to Living the Old Ways* by Edain McCoy
+ *The Stations of the Sun* by Ronald Hutton

tools of the trade
+ *Wicca: A Guide for the Solitary Practitioner* by Scott Cunningham
+ *Buckland's Complete Book of Witchcraft* by Raymond Buckland
+ *Besom, Stang & Sword* by Christopher Orapello

the elements
+ *Earth Power: Techniques of Nature* by Scott Cunningham
+ *Air Magic* by Astrea Taylor
+ *Fire Magic* by Josephine Winter

+ *Water Magic* by Lilith Dorsey
+ *Earth Magic* by Dodie Graham McKay

crystals
+ *The Crystal Bible* by Judy Hall
+ *Crystal Grids Handbook* by Judy Hall

herbs
+ *The Modern Witchcraft Guide to Magickal Herbs* by Judy Ann Nock
+ *Plant Witchery* by Juliet Diaz
+ *The Encyclopedia of Magical Herbs* by Scott Cunningham

candle magick
+ *The Book of Candle Magic* by Madame Pamita
+ *Lighting the Wick* by Sandra Mariah Wright and Leanne Marrama

divination
+ *Seventy-Eight Degrees of Wisdom* by Rachel Pollack
+ *Learning Lenormand* by Marcus Katz
+ *The Modern Witchcraft Book of Tarot* by Skye Alexander

astrology
+ *Astrology for Real Life* by Theresa Reed
+ *Chart Interpretation Handbook* by Stephen Arroyo
+ *The Twelve Houses* by Howard Sasportas
+ *Aspects in Astrology* by Sue Tompkins

spells
+ *The Modern Witchcraft Spell Book* by Skye Alexander
+ *Spellcrafting* by Arin Murphy-Hiscock

everyDay maɢick

+ *The Witch's Book of Self Care* by Arin Murphy-Hiscock
+ *Glamour Magic* by Deborah Castellano
+ *Everyday Witchcraft* by Deborah Blake

witch types

+ *The Path of the Witch* by Lidia Pradas
+ *The Green Witch* by Arin-Murphy Hiscock
+ *The House Witch* by Arin-Murphy Hiscock

BIBLIOGRAPHY

Becker, Marshall J. "An American Witch Bottle." Archaeology. archive.archaeology
.org/online/features/halloween/witch_bottle.html.

Berard, Adrienne. "Civil War-Era Bottle Found on Highway Median May
Be Rare 'Witch Bottle.'" William & Mary, January 22, 2020. https://www
.wm.edu/news/stories/2020/civil-war-era-jug-found-on-highway-median
-may-be-rare-witch-bottle.php.

Blake, Deborah. *Midsummer: Rituals, Recipes & Lore for Litha*. Woodbury, MN:
Llewellyn Publications, 2015.

Buckland, Raymond. *Buckland's Complete Book of Witchcraft*. St. Paul, MN:
Llewellyn Publications, 1986.

Cartwright, Mark. "Lugh." World History Encyclopedia, January 29, 2021.
https://www.worldhistory.org/Lugh/.

Cole, Stephanie. "Is Glass Biodegradable & Is It Better than Plastic?" The Roundup.
Accessed October 12, 2022. https://theroundup.org/is-glass-biodegradable/.

Connor, Kerri. *Ostara: Rituals, Recipes & Lore for the Spring Equinox*. Woodbury,
MN: Llewellyn Publications, 2015.

Cunningham, Scott. *Cunningham's Encyclopedia of Magical Herbs*. St. Paul, MN:
Llewellyn Publications, 2000. See esp. "Folk Names Cross-Reference."

———. *Wicca: A Guide for the Solitary Practitioner*. St. Paul, MN: Llewellyn
Publications, 2010.

Daley, Jason. "'Witch Bottle' Filled with Teeth, Pins and Mysterious Liquid Discovered in English Chimney." *Smithsonian Magazine*, November 1, 2019. https://www.smithsonianmag.com/smart-news/witch-bottle-full-teeth-pins -and-possibly-urine-discovered-chimney-180973448/.

"A Detailed History of Beltane." Beltane Fire Society, March 25, 2015. https:// beltane.org/a-detailed-history-of-beltane/.

The Editors of *Encyclopaedia Britannica*. "Hellebore." Britannica. Updated October 8, 2013. https://www.britannica.com/plant/hellebore.

Fields, Douglas R. *Electric Brain*. Dallas: BenBella Books, 2020. Kindle.

Fordham, Frieda, Michael S. M. Fordham, and the Editors of *Encyclopaedia Britannica*. "Carl Jung." Britannica. Updated July 22, 2022. https://www.britannica .com/biography/Carl-Jung.

Groeneveld, Emma. "Runes." World History Encyclopedia, June 19, 2018. https://www.worldhistory.org/runes/.

Hall, Judy. *The Crystal Bible: A Definitive Guide to Crystals*. New York: Penguin Random House, 2003.

History.com Editors. "Imbolc." History. Updated February 1, 2021. https://www .history.com/topics/holidays/imbolc.

———. "May Day." History. Updated April 29, 2021. https://www.history.com /topics/holidays/history-of-may-day.

———. "Samhain." History. Updated October 19, 2021. https://www.history .com/topics/holidays/samhain.

———. "Saturnalia." History. Updated December 18, 2020. https://www.history .com/topics/ancient-rome/saturnalia.

———. "Summer Solstice." History. Updated August 21, 2018. https://www history.com/topics/natural-disasters-and-environment/history-of-summer -solstice.

———. "Winter Solstice." History. Updated December 21, 2020. https://www .history.com/topics/natural-disasters-and-environment/winter-solstice.

Inkwright, Fez. *Botanical Curses and Poisons: The Shadow-Lives of Plants*. London: Liminal 11, 2021.

Jung, Carl G. *Man and His Symbols*. Garden City, NY: Doubleday, 1964.

———. *The Archetypes and the Collective Unconscious*. Vol. 9 , Part 1 of *The Collected Works of C. G. Jung*, edited by Gerhard Adler, Michael Fordham, Sir Herbert Read, and William McGuire. Translated by R. F. C. Hull. Princeton, NJ: Princeton University Press, 1990.

Kelly, Aidan. "About Naming Ostara, Litha, and Mabon." *Including Paganism with Aidan Kelley: Expanding Dialogue on World Religions* (blog). Patheos, May 2, 2017. https://www.patheos.com/blogs/aidankelly/2017/05/naming -ostara-litha-mabon/.

Leopold, Susan. "What Is Going On with White Sage?" United Plant Savers, June 24, 2019. https://unitedplantsavers.org/what-is-going-on-with-white-sage/.

Mankey, Jason. *Witch's Wheel of the Year: Rituals for Circles, Solitaries & Covens*. Woodbury, MN: Llewellyn Publications, 2019.

Mark, Joshua J. "Wheel of The Year." World History Encyclopedia, January 28, 2019. https://www.worldhistory.org/Wheel_of_the_Year/.

Michael, Coby. *The Poison Path Herbal: Baneful Herbs, Medicinal Nightshades, and Ritual Entheogens*. Rochester, VT: Park Street Press, 2021.

"The Mohs Hardness Scale and Chart for Select Gems." International Gem Society. Accessed July 9, 2021. https://www.gemsociety.org/article/select-gems -ordered-mohs-hardness/.

Neal, Carl F. *Imbolc: Rituals, Recipes & Lore for Brigid's Day*. Woodbury, MN: Llewellyn Publications, 2015.

Pesznecker, Susan. *Yule: Rituals, Recipes & Lore for the Winter Solstice*. Woodbury, MN: Llewellyn Publications, 2015.

Powell, Alvin. "When Science Meets Mindfulness: Researchers Study How It Seems to Change the Brain in Depressed Patients." *Harvard Gazette*, April 9, 2018. https://news.harvard.edu/gazette/story/2018/04/harvard-researchers -study-how-mindfulness-may-change-the-brain-in-depressed-patients/.

"The Powerful Solanaceae." United States Department of Agriculture. Accessed June 22, 2022. https://www.fs.usda.gov/wildflowers/ethnobotany/Mind_and _Spirit/solanaceae.shtml.

Rajchel, Diana. *Mabon: Rituals, Recipes & Lore for the Autumn Equinox*. Woodbury, MN: Llewellyn Publications, 2015.

———. *Samhain: Rituals, Recipes, & Lore for Halloween*. Woodbury, MN: Llewellyn Publications, 2015.

Rehman, Sumbul. "Old.amu.ac.in." Solanaceae Nightshades Family. Accessed June 23, 2022. https://old.amu.ac.in/emp/studym/100007806.pdf.

Smith, Lori. "What Are Binaural Beats, and How Do They Work?" Edited by Andrew Gonzales. Medical News Today, September 30, 2019. https://www .medicalnewstoday.com/articles/320019#benefits.

Stanborough, Rebecca Joy. "A Hobby for All Seasons: 7 Science-Backed Benefits of Indoor Plants." Edited by Deborah Weatherspoon. Healthline, September 18, 2020. https://www.healthline.com/health/healthy-home-guide /benefits-of-indoor-plants#safe-plants.

Ward, Coby Michael. "A Collection of Mandrake Folklore." *Poisoner's Apothecary* (blog). *Patheos*, March 26, 2018. https://www.patheos.com/blogs/poisoners apothecary/2018/03/26/a-collection-of-mandrake-folklore/.

———. "The Court of Helleborus: A Collection of Hellebore Lore." *Poisoner's Apothecary* (blog). *Patheos*, June 11, 2018. https://www.patheos.com/blogs /poisonersapothecary/2018/06/11/the-court-of-helleborus-a-collection-of -hellebore-lore/.

———. "Devil's Apple: A Collection of Datura Folklore." *Poisoner's Apothecary* (blog). *Patheos*, June 4, 2018. https://www.patheos.com/blogs/poisoners apothecary/2018/06/04/devils-apple-a-collection-of-datura-folklore/.

Water Science School. "The Water in You: Water and the Human Body." USGS, May 22, 2019. https://www.usgs.gov/special-topics/water-science-school /science/water-you-water-and-human-body.

"What Is Energy?" US Energy Information Administration. Updated December 13, 2021. https://www.eia.gov/energyexplained/what-is-energy/.

Wigington, Patti. "Magical Herbal Correspondences." Learn Religions. Updated June 25, 2019. https://www.learnreligions.com/magical-herb-correspondences -4064512.

————. "Beltane History – Celebrating May Day." Learn Religions. Updated February 3, 2020. https://www.learnreligions.com/the-history-of-beltane-and -may-day-2561657.

————. "History of Yule." Learn Religions. Updated June 25, 2019. https:// www.learnreligions.com/history-of-yule-2562997.

"'Witch Bottles' Concealed and Revealed." MOLA. Accessed March 3, 2022. https://www.mola.org.uk/witch-bottles-concealed-and-revealed.